Collecting
Rhead Pottery
Charlotte
Frederick • Frederick Hurten

Bernard Bumpus

Francis Joseph

ISBN 1-870703-08-1

Acknowledgements

In the acknowledgements which appeared in Charlotte Rhead: Potter and Designer, 1987, I listed the many people who had helped with my research. At the head was Katherine Rhead, Sister St. Pierre, Charlotte's last surviving sister. Sadly she is no longer with us as she died a few months after her hundredth birthday in 1987. I am still most grateful for her help she gave me, which has been of enduring value, as I am to the many other members of the Rhead family who provided information about Charlotte and her relatives.

People who knew or worked with Charlotte Rhead and who contributed in many ways to my original book included Mr Ernest Bailey, Mrs. Catherine Barlow, Mr. F. Capey, Mrs. Rose Cumberbatch, Mrs. Nora Dobbs, Mrs. May Doorbar, Miss Mary Harper, Mrs. Nellie Hill, Mr. Albert Litherland, Mr. D. H. Lowe, Mr. & Mrs. W. Mack, Mrs. Rose Platt, Mrs. Nora Shreyhane, and Mr. Tom Whalley. Also Mr. M. L. Aaron, Mrs. E. Capper, Mr. Barry Leigh, Mr. Edmund Leigh, Mr. Francis Wood, Major Paul Wood, and Mr. Tony Wood.

Others who helped my research included Margaret Birks, Brian Boyd, Joan Jackson, Beatrice Moorcroft, Barbara Morris, Pam Rigby, Eva Walters and Sylvia and Edmund Yorke. Over the past ten years I have received many letters containing valuable new information and I am most grateful to all of those who have written, sent photographs, or turned up fresh facts. Among them I must mention Patrick Beasley, Beverley and Beth, John R. Burton, Janet Gatley, Peter Freeman, Rodney and Eileen Hampson, Bill Jones, Anne Lemon, Malcolm and Jane, Michael of Hertford Antiques, John C. F. Phillipps, Mabel Rowley (Mrs. Mabel Smith), Lynn Scholz, Bob and Trudy Share, Peter Shilton, Sally Strosnider, Pat Watson, and D. W. Williams.

Particular thanks are due to Eddie Sambrook, who has provided much firsthand information about the work of Frederick Rhead and Charlotte Rhead at the Wood potteries, to Dora Shaw, and to Gerrard Shaw for his valuable insights into the A. G. Richardson productions and his comments on the relevant chapter of this book. His book, now in preparation, on Richardson's print and enamelled patterns of the 1920s and 1930s, a development of his MA dissertation, will include much material on Charlotte Rhead's tableware not covered here.

I am particularly grateful to Miranda Goodby, Keeper of Ceramics at the City Museum and Art Gallery, Stoke-on-Trent and to her staff, especially for making available the Richardson pattern books.

Finally I must thank my family for their patience and for much encouragement and constructive advice.

To Judith

© 1999 Francis Joseph Publications

ISBN 1-870703-08-1

Published by Francis Joseph,
5 Southbrook Mews, London SE12 8LG
Telephone 0208 318 9580

Photographs: Trevor Leek

Scanning: Gabriel Granger

Typesetting by
E J Folkard Print Services
199 Station Road, Crayford, Kent DA1 3QF

Printed by Greenwich Press Ltd
Eastmoor Street, London SE7 8LX

Front cover photograph: Burgess & Leigh pattern 4111.

Contents

Introduction

This book builds on my *Charlotte Rhead: Potter and Designer* which was published twelve years ago and is now out of print. During the period much new information has emerged about the work of Frederick and Charlotte Rhead during the first part of the century. Most significantly, nearly all of the Richardson Pattern Books which cover the time that Charlotte Rhead worked for the company during the 1930s have recently become available, enabling the chapter on her work for Richardsons (Crown Ducal) to be rewritten and a near definitive list of commercially produced patterns compiled.

An additional chapter has been added on the Rhead's tile productions. The chapter on Wood and Sons and Bursley Ltd. has been greatly enlarged so as to take in the decorative designs of Frederick Rhead as well as those of Charlotte, thus catering for the increasing number of collectors with an interest in his work. These additions are logical as Charlotte cooperated closely with her father, the company art director, and worked in an adjoining office. There must have been many exchanges of ideas between father and daughter and indeed it is not always easy to determine who did what. Although the company pattern books of the period do not appear to have survived, some of the section books of the time, giving details of patterns – mainly of tableware – sent for engraving, are still extant and provide useful data. The lists of the Wood & Sons and Bursley Ltd. patterns include all those known to me though there are still many gaps, particularly in the Bursley section, which need to be filled.

The Burgess & Leigh and H. J. Wood Ltd. patterns have also been revised and now incorporate all the new information that has come to light in the past twelve years. In this connection I am most grateful to the many people who have written and have sent photographs of unusual pieces. I would of course continue to welcome new information about any of the Rhead productions of the period. Letters should be sent to me via the publisher of this book, Francis Joseph.

The principal trade magazines consulted remain *The Pottery Gazette* and *The Pottery and Glass Record*. In the references to these magazines that follow I have used the abbreviations *PG* and *PGR*. All quoted descriptions in the lists of patterns are taken from these two sources.

The values in this book are not those of the author and are compiled from reliable sources including auctioneers, antique dealers and collectors.

CHAPTER ONE
The Rhead Family

Fig 1 George Woolliscroft Rhead senior and his wife Fanny. This pâte-sur-pâte plaque was Frederick Rhead's gift to his parents on the occasion of their Golden Wedding in 1904.

The Rheads, an old North Staffordshire family, had been connected with pots and potting since the eighteenth century and possibly longer, but there was little in the family history to suggest that they had any special artistic talents. Matters were to change with the birth in 1832 of George Woolliscroft Rhead as he proved to be the first of a line, which was to run through three generations, of uncommonly gifted artists. His talents were first displayed when he was a young apprentice in the highly skilled gilding trade. In due course he was appointed a gilder at Minton's, later promoted to be their heraldic gilder at a time when Minton's reputation was at its peak. Its productions, under the artistic direction of Léon Arnoux, were sought by royalty and the wealthy throughout the world.

George Woolliscroft was also prominent as an art educator. After serving for ten years as Assistant Master at the Newcastle-under-Lyme Art School, he became Master of the art classes at Chesterton, Fenton and Longton, positions he continued to hold until he retired in 1900. He was a deeply religious man and regarded conducting Sunday School classes as a natural extension of his teaching. He was, it seems, so well acquainted with the Bible that his grandchildren believed that he knew it off by heart!

In 1854 he married Fanny Colley (Fig 1), a Shropshire girl from Broseley, who may also have had pottery connections. Of their eleven children, five, the eldest, George Woolliscroft junior, Frederick Alfred, Louis John, Fanny, and Alice inherited their father's artistic talents in one way or another and for a time at least followed the family calling as potters. Bertrand, the youngest child, while not a potter, held a string of important posts in the pottery lithographic trade both in England and the United States and also wrote knowledgeably about the industry.

While in their teens George, Frederick, Louis and Alice all became apprentices at Minton's, though the form each apprenticeship took varied. The artist W. S. Coleman had joined Minton's in 1869 and George junior was assigned to his studio 'for the purpose of giving him instruction in the practical working of pot colours'.[1] Two years later, when Minton's Art-Pottery Studio was set up in Kensington Gore in

Fig 2 Josiah Wedgwood & Sons, 'Longfellow' Jug, 1880. The etching of the poet was made by George Woolliscroft Rhead jr.

London – a joint venture between the company and the government – with Coleman as art director, George went with him to work as a pottery painter. Coleman left after a year or two but George remained at the Studio until it burnt down in 1875 when he returned to the Potteries. He was back in London two years later, having won a scholarship to the South Kensington School of Art (now a post-graduate school, the Royal College of Art). While he was there he was awarded several prizes and stayed on for an additional year in order to qualify for an Art Class Teaching Certificate. At the School he also studied etching under Alphonse Legros, the Slade Professor of Fine Art at University College. He must also have become proficient in French as Legros, despite being a naturalised British citizen, would not speak English.

George then put his French to good use, spending some time in France and visiting Italy, before settling in London permanently. He was something of a polymath, painting, etching, designing stained glass, writing and teaching, eventually becoming head of the Putney Borough Polytechnic and the Norwood Schools of Art. He continued to find an outlet for the skills he had learned at Minton's since he occasionally worked as a freelance faience painter for Doulton's in Lambeth. Wedgwood also put his talents to good use, employing him to make etchings of celebrated figures which were applied to commemorative wares. The first of these, of the poet Longfellow, was intended for a jug for the American market (Fig 2), though later etchings were made for Wedgwood's home trade and included portraits of Thomas Carlyle, Benjamin Disraeli and Queen Victoria.

Louis Rhead, the third son, was sent to Paris at the age of 13 for three years to study figure drawing with the artist Gustave Boulanger, probably at *L'Académie Julian*. On his return to Stoke in 1873, he was apprenticed as a painter at Minton's. Early in 1878 he joined Wedgwood's where,

Fig 3 Josiah Wedgwood & Sons. Plaque painted by Louis Rhead and exhibited at the 1878 Paris Universal Exhibition. From The Art Journal.

quickly making his mark, he decorated several works which the company exhibited at the Paris Universal Exhibition that year. One of these pieces, a plaque (Fig 3), attracted this comment from a trade paper:

'Mr.L.Rhead has a Persian plaque with a lady kneeling and painting a vase. The drawing is in strong outline, and the colouring of the flesh is conventional . . . Many who have seen this piece will be inclined to doubt whether it has been entirely composed and painted by this young artist (he cannot be above 18 years of age) but such is nevertheless a fact'.[2]

A few months later Louis, too, was awarded a scholarship to the South Kensington School of Art and, like his brother George, he remained in London after the course had ended. He continued to work for Wedgwood's as a freelance, mainly, it seems, painting faience plaques. The example illustrated in Fig 4 is probably fairly typical as the company had suggested to him 'that a pretty girl, or woman & child is always more taking than any other subject'.[3] In 1883 he accepted an offer from the American publisher D. Appleton to become the company art director in New York and he left England for good, soon taking American citizenship. He is best known now for the Art Nouveau posters which he designed in the 1890s, one of which, an 1894 advertisement for the American journal *The Sun* (Fig 5), was copied by several Staffordshire potteries (Fig 6). Other designs by Louis were adapted by his brother Frederick, mainly on the popular *Intarsio* ware which Frederick developed when he was art director of the firm of Wileman & Co (Fig 7).

Fanny Rhead married and her eleven children left her no time to pursue a full-time career but she still managed to paint and design (and to teach dancing), while working as a freelance. Some of the most unusual turn-of-the-century productions of the Fenton firm Robinson & Son (later renamed E. Brain & Co.) were her work, among them twelve 'Egyptian' designs, part of the *Harjian* series (Fig 8). As for Alice, she, too, was apprenticed for a time as an enamel ware decorator at Minton's though little is known about her work. She married three times, and presumably had no opportunity or inclination to pursue a career in the Potteries.

Fig 4 Josiah Wedgwood & Sons. Faience plaque painted by Louis Rhead, c1880. Phillips.

It was Frederick Alfred Rhead, the second child, who was to follow the traditional family rôle of potter

Fig 5 Louis Rhead, poster for the American journal The Sun, 1894.

Fig 6 Louis Rhead's poster design illustrated in Fig 5 was copied by several English potteries. This example was made by the British Anchor Pottery, c1900.

Fig 7 Intarsio Ewer, pattern no. 3053, Wileman & Co. Adapted by Frederick Rhead from a design by his brother Louis Rhead, c1898.

and combine it with that of artist, designer and writer. He was born in 1856 in Newcastle-under-Lyme. When he was thirteen he joined Minton's as an apprentice painter, and around the same time began to attend evening classes at the Newcastle School of Art where his father was Assistant Master. A year later Frederick was fortunate to be assigned as an apprentice to the French ceramist and sculptor Louis Solon. Widely regarded as the leading exponent of the difficult decorative technique *pâte-sur-pâte*,[4] Solon had worked for thirteen years at the Imperial Porcelain Manufactory at Sèvres. He came to England in October 1870 during the Franco-Prussian War, the Sèvres Manufactory having been closed and the town evacuated in the face of the advancing Prussian army. Frederick worked for Solon until December 1877, by which time he himself had thoroughly mastered the *pâte-sur-pâte* technique (Fig 9).

Minton's also employed several other continental artists and in this cosmopolitan milieu Frederick was introduced to the Hürten family. C. F. Hürten, a German from Cologne, was a superb naturalistic flower painter who had come to Sèvres where he had married a local girl. In 1869 he was persuaded to join W. T. Copeland in England, his works exhibited at the 1867 Paris Universal Exhibition having been much admired by Alderman Copeland, the firm's head. Frederick fell in love with Hürten's younger daughter, Adolphine, a beautiful girl and an amateur singer and actress. As the Hürtens were Catholics and Frederick a Protestant, there were obstacles to the marriage which were only overcome when papal dispensation was obtained. Although Frederick himself did not convert, the wedding eventually took place in the Dominican church in Stoke-on-Trent and the six children of the marriage were brought up as Catholics.

Until his death in 1933, Frederick worked almost continuously in the Potteries as an artist and designer. At Minton's several of his *pâte-sur-pâte*

Fig 8 E. Brain & Co., vase for the Harjian series designed by Fanny Rhead, c1903.

Fig 9 Minton, bottle decorated in pâte-sur-pâte by Frederick Rhead, 1875.

designs, some featuring cattle or other animals, showed features and originality at a period when Classical or Oriental motifs were the convention. Early in 1878 he and his brother Louis both joined Wedgwood's, and, like Louis, his work shown at the Paris Universal Exhibition that year was acclaimed in the trade press. Among his designs exhibited there was a bottle decorated in sgraffito with an Egyptian head (Fig 10), now in the British Museum.[5] His eclecticism as a designer at this time is demonstrated by the large 'aesthetic' vase illustrated in Fig 11 which he painted about the same time for the firm of Pinder, Bourne in Burslem, presumably as a freelance.

Fig 10 Josiah Wedgwood & Son, pilgrim bottle with sgraffito decoration designed by Frederick Rhead. It was exhibited at the Paris Universal Exhibition in 1878. The British Museum.

After leaving Wedgwood, Frederick Rhead worked first as art director for the firm of James Gildea and then moved to a similar post with E. J. D. Bodley. Bodley was a staunch Liberal and made Frederick available in 1887 to design and decorate the monumental *pâte-sur-pâte* Gladstone Vase (Fig 12).[6] Commissioned by the Burslem Liberals, it was presented to the former Liberal politician and sometime Prime Minister, W. E. Gladstone, out of office at the time, at his home, Hawarden Castle, in 1888. After Bodley's, Frederick was appointed art director for the Brownfield Guild Pottery and, from around 1897 to 1905, for Wileman & Co. where he introduced the well-known *Intarsio* ware. His designs for Wileman's are popular with collectors and are well documented[7] as many of the company pattern books have survived, but a detailed account of these productions is beyond the scope of this book. In 1905 Frederick worked for a time as a freelance consulting designer before becoming a partner in his own tile manufacturing firm, Barker, Rhead, in 1908 (Chapter Three). When this enterprise failed in 1910 he went to the United States, but could not settle there and returned to England after only eleven months. He soon found a new job, and early in 1912 he joined Wood & Sons as the company art director, a position he held until 1929 (see Chapter Four) when he took up a similar post at Cauldon Potteries. At the time Cauldon was a large conglomerate which included Royal Crown Derby, Royal Worcester and Ridgways (Bedford Works), where Frederick had his office. While at Cauldon he became seriously ill, and in 1933 he died.

Fig 11 Pinder, Bourne & Co., vase with painted decoration by Frederick Rhead, c1880.

Fig 12 'The Gladstone Vase', designed and executed by Frederick Rhead, 1887. The vase, commissioned by the Burslem Liberals, was presented to the former prime minister W. E. Gladstone in August 1888 at his home, Hawarden Castle.

Of his children, the two boys, Frederick Hurten and Harry, born respectively in 1880 and 1882, and two of the girls, Charlotte, born in 1885 and Adolphine, born three years later, were all involved in the pottery industry. But Adolphine, familiarly known as Dollie or Dolly (confusingly she seems to have used both spellings), stayed for only a relatively short period and sometime around 1910 left the Potteries to train as a midwife. The other two girls both became teachers, Katherine, the younger, later taking the veil with the name Sister St. Pierre. She joined the Ursulines, a French teaching order which had houses in England at the time. When these were closed, she moved to France where she remained for the rest of her life.

The boys served their apprenticeship with their father at Brownfield's which made a wide range of goods of excellent quality, and where they obtained a thorough grounding in their trade. They also attended evening classes at the Wedgwood Institute, Burslem, and at the Government Art Schools in Stoke-on-Trent, Fenton and Longton. After Brownfield's they both went to work for their father at Wileman & Co. when Frederick was appointed art director around 1897. Their subsequent careers are described in Chapter Two.

SKELETON FAMILY TREE

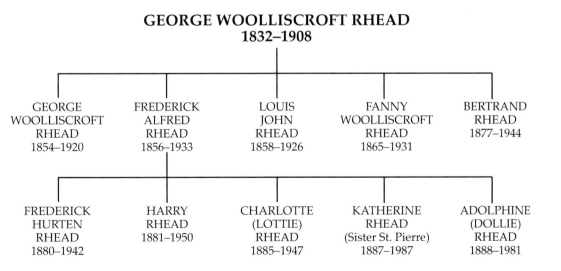

This is not a full family tree of the Rheads but a key to the relationship of the members of the family mentioned in this book.

CHAPTER TWO

Charlotte Rhead and her Brothers and Sisters

Charlotte Rhead was born in Burslem on 19th October 1885 at 12, Newport Street, the fourth child and second daughter of Frederick and Adolphine Rhead. She was christened Charlotte Antoinette Adolphine but was always known to her family and friends as Lottie, a first name she also used professionally until the 1930s. Then, towards the end of 1932, she changed to the more formal 'Charlotte', presumably because she felt this was more in accord with her growing status and reputation (Fig 13).

12 Newport Street was a small, two storied house with only three bedrooms, a kitchen and living room, and front and back yards. The neighbours would have been a mixture of pottery designers and decorators, workmen of various kinds and tradesmen. Like most property of this kind, the Rhead's house was rented.

Fig 13 A Rhead family group photographed in the 1930s. Charlotte is seated in the front with her mother behind her on her left.

The Rhead family had moved to Burslem in about 1881, probably because Frederick had been appointed art director for the firm of Gildea at the Dale Hall Pottery. They remained there for about nine years when another small house was rented in London Road, Stoke. By this time Frederick was working both part-time for Brownfield's at Cobridge and as a freelance designer. As the six towns which comprised the Potteries were several miles apart and public transport limited, Stoke was now a more convenient location for him. It was here that Lottie started attending the local kindergarten school.

In 1892, when she was seven, she was struck down with a gastric complaint and had to be moved into her parents' bedroom so that she could be nursed night and day. When at last she was well enough to go out, she was knocked over by a boy and broke her thigh, and again she was bedridden. When the thigh mended, one leg was found to be longer than the other which gave her a limp. The doctor resorted to a primitive form of traction. He put her to bed once more, tied a brick to the shorter leg which he hung over the end of the bed and instructed her to bear this painful device for several hours each day. Surprisingly the treatment worked, and eventually she was able to walk normally. These illnesses and mishaps delayed her formal education and set her back considerably. She was in any case a slow learner and particularly weak in mathematics.

About 1894 the family was able to move away from the smoky atmosphere of Stoke to a small village. Frederick, now promoted to the post of art director at Brownfield's, rented a newly-built six-roomed semi-detached house in Porthill, between Newcastle and Longport, at the time quite a rural area. Here the young Rheads at last had space. With playing fields nearby, they joined the local children in various games, including cricket and football.

On Saturday mornings the oldest boy, Frederick Hurten, took charge and went for walks with Charlotte and the other girls in the surrounding country. A favourite spot was Bradwell Wood – now a housing estate – where they would pick bluebells in the spring. On one of these walks on a July morning Charlotte climbed a tree overlooking a pond to get a better view of some fishermen, slipped and fell in. The others managed to rescue her, but afraid of their mother's reaction, they undressed her, wrapped her in a coat and laid out her clothes in the sun. Fortunately it was a hot day and by the time they got home, the clothes were nearly dry. It was some weeks before Mrs. Rhead learned of the mishap from a cousin. Her father, Frederick Alfred, was a keen fisherman and he would sometimes take Charlotte or one of his other daughters with him on fishing expeditions. These outings were less popular though, as there was a strict requirement to keep quiet and still.

Other family diversions included amateur theatricals, the plays sometimes being written by Frederick Rhead himself. One such was about an articulated doll in which Charlotte was cast in the leading role.

A grand performance, in fancy dress, was staged in the dining room and her acting won general acclaim. Perhaps she took after her mother who had been a talented amateur actress before her marriage.

The move to Porthill brought a change in the educational arrangements for Charlotte and her sisters, all four transferring to the Longport School. This was some distance from their home, so their brother Frederick Hurten, who was now apprenticed to his father at Brownfield's, took them to school in the morning on his way to work. Lunch was taken with the school caretaker, a widow, Mrs. Coin, who warmed up the food provided by Mrs. Rhead and added some potatoes – all for sixpence a week.

At first the girls were placed in different classes, Charlotte's being Standard III. Homework consisted mainly of spelling practice, for which the words to be learned were noted on the pupils' slates. The sisters went home together, trying out their spelling on the way, paying particular attention to the words that Charlotte had to learn. History does not record whether or not her education was helped by the family parrot. This remarkable bird could, it seems, recite the alphabet and then repeat it backwards.

About this time her father, an experienced art school instructor, started teaching Charlotte drawing and painting. Frederick often carried on his business at home, working on some new designs perhaps or decorating a vase or plaque in *pâte-sur-pâte*, a technique he had learned in the 1870s at Minton's during his apprenticeship to Louis Solon. Occasionally Charlotte and the other children might serve as models. By watching him at work Charlotte must have learned a great deal about a technique which she later practised herself.

The girls remained at the Longport School for four years. Despite an excellent headmaster who himself taught mathematics, Charlotte remained weak in the subject, and although she progressed to Standard IV, she had to remain in the class for two years. By the time she had moved up to Standard V, her younger sister, Katherine, had caught up with her.

However, at this point the family left Porthill as Frederick senior had obtained a new job in Fenton, as art director of Wileman & Company – later to be renamed the Shelley Potteries. So another and larger house was rented, at 28 Regent Road. It had four bedrooms and a bathroom, the latter something of a luxury for the Rheads although it only provided cold running water. There followed too the inevitable educational upheaval and it was decided that Charlotte should attend the Hanley Higher Grade School. This involved a three mile walk, but her close friend Lena Massey was already a pupil there and the two girls used to go together. Charlotte's leg was giving her no trouble and there was a tram service which could be used in bad weather or in an emergency. At Hanley Charlotte was placed in Standard VI. The school was modern and lit by electricity, a novelty at a time when gas was still the normal method of lighting. Katherine soon joined her at the school and in 1899 the sisters were both promoted to Standard VII. However, the going proved tough for Charlotte, and Katherine, who excelled in mathematics, had to give her a great deal of help.

Sometime around the turn of the century and towards the end of Charlotte's school career, her father Frederick introduced the decorative technique of tube-lining at Wileman's. This process, which requires considerable control, makes use of a technique similar to icing a cake. It is described in the Appendix. Tube-lining had been introduced to the Potteries by Harry Barnard in 1895. Barnard, a sculptor by training, had come to the Potteries from Doulton's in Lambeth to set up an art pottery department for the firm of Macintyre's in Burslem. He soon moved on to Wedgwood's, which for a few years also took up tube-lining. When the company decided to give up the process, Barnard asked Frederick Rhead to take over the girls he had trained. So it was that Wileman's introduced its own tube-lined range (Plates 1, 2 and 114). Charlotte's two brothers both worked at Wileman's and they became proficient in the technique which they taught to Charlotte and Dollie, the youngest sister, both of whom became highly successful tube-liners (Plates 3 and 5).

Charlotte left the Hanley Higher Grade School in the spring of 1900. In that year a large exhibition, running from May until November, was held at Earls Court in London. Wileman's took a stand there, mainly to display and sell Frederick's most successful line, *Intarsio*. Each piece of this ware was decorated with a printed outline which was then coloured by hand

Fig 14 Intarsio clock, Wileman & Co., pattern no. 3329. Designed by Frederick Rhead. c1900. Value £1000/$1800.

13

and glazed (Fig 14). The unusual designs, many of them humorous, were very advanced for their day and among the shops that stocked the range was Liberty's of Regent Street. Mrs. Rhead had agreed to look after the Wileman stand at the exhibition and she took Charlotte to London to help her, the two of them staying with Mrs. Rhead's sister in Kilburn. They travelled to Earls Court each day on the Underground, newly opened at that time. Frederick came to London at weekends to keep an eye on things and to make sure there was enough stock to meet the substantial sales. Charlotte must have enjoyed the experience as she had the run of the exhibition itself, as well as a wonderful opportunity to see something of the sights of London.

Fig 15 Charlotte Rhead, design for a tobacco jar, from the American Arts & Crafts magazine Keramic Studio, December 1905.

Although Charlotte's formal schooling was over, her art education had barely begun. After she returned from London she enrolled with Dollie at the Fenton Art School. This school had been established by her grandfather George Woolliscroft Rhead in 1889 and at the time she joined, its reputation and influence was growing under the direction of a new Principal, W. Morse. Among other subjects, the School taught the girls enamelling, a skill which added to their already considerable abilities as tube-liners. The prevailing decorative style at the time was Art Nouveau. Despite being derided in the Potteries as 'New Art', it was nevertheless widely adopted, not least by Minton's whose popular tube-lined range, appropriately named *Secessionist Ware*, was selling well. The long and sinuous trailing forms, so characteristic of the Art Nouveau style, and reminiscent of organic growths, must have made Charlotte look at the plant forms around her with new eyes. No doubt she was also encouraged to try her hand at designing, inspired by the family tradition and by what she

Fig 16 Thomas Forester, plaque painted by Frederick Hurten Rhead, c1900.

had seen at the Earls Court exhibition. One of her patterns, for a tobacco jar in the *Intarsio* style, was later illustrated in the American Arts and Crafts magazine *Keramic Studio* (Fig 15).

In 1899, when he was only nineteen, Charlotte's elder brother, Frederick Hurten, was appointed art director of Wardle & Co., a small but well regarded art pottery in Hanley. This must have been a part-time job as he was still working for his father at Wileman's and also for Thomas Forester, another art pottery. At Forester's he was employed as a decorator, his designs there were tubed or painted, some with exotic birds usually in a vaguely Japanese setting (Fig 16), others with swirling art nouveauish plant forms, while others again featured designs after Walter Crane. The Forester jardinière base in Fig 17 for instance is a copy of Crane's illustration *Pandora desires to open the box* from the 1892 edition of Nathaniel Hawthorne's *Wonder Book for Girls and Boys*. Frederick Hurten was an admirer of Crane and Crane's influence on his designs for Wardle's and later in the United States is apparent.

Fig 17 Thomas Forester jardinière stand, painted by Frederick Hurten Rhead after Walter Crane's illustration Pandora Seeks to Open the Box. From Hawthorne's 'A Wonder Book of Girls and Boys', 1892 edition.

Although Frederick Hurten was nominally the Wardle art director, it is likely that his father had a watching brief over the operation as the company also started marketing tube-lined wares, some of them with patterns bearing a remarkable likeness to the Wileman tube-lined range. This technique was becoming increasingly popular and it was particularly suitable for decorating the contemporary Art Nouveau wares.

The Rhead family became further involved with Wardle's when Charlotte joined the firm in 1901, probably as a tube-liner and enameller, Dollie following her a year or two later. The jardinière (Plate 3) and the candlestick tubed with a pattern of swimming fish (Plate 4) seem likely to be their work and the designs can confidently be attributed to one of the Rheads, most probably Frederick Hurten. But in the summer of 1902 Frederick Hurten resigned from Wardle's to take up a post in the United States. The immediate reason for his departure may have been his marriage to Agnes, a paintress from the shop floor, an event that was regarded with considerable dismay by the family at the time. The marriage itself took place on Boxing Day, 1901 and the only other Rhead present

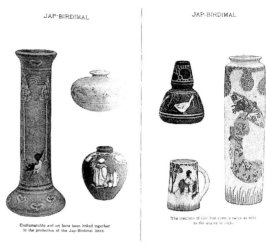

Fig 18 Examples of Jap-Birdimal Ware from a Weller Pottery catalogue, c1904.

seems to have been Frederick Hurten's uncle, Bertrand. He was the youngest of George Woolliscroft's eleven children and was only a few years older than his nephew, so he may have felt more sympathy for him than the other members of the family. The rather odd circumstances surrounding the marriage suggest that somehow Frederick Hurten was either forced or tricked into it.

On arrival in the United States Frederick Hurten joined the small Avon pottery in Tiltonville, Ohio, a job that must have been arranged for him by another English employee there, W. P. Jervis. Jervis had worked at Minton's in the 1870s, probably in an administrative capacity, where he had become friendly with the Rhead family, but had emigrated to America around 1890. In Tiltonville Frederick Hurten soon introduced tube-lining, known locally as the 'squeeze bag' technique and the designs on the relatively few productions from this period that survive reflect his English background and training. Stylised flower-heads and sinuous plant forms predominate while some pieces feature tubed mottoes, a typical Arts and Crafts device. One vase decorated with dandelions was nostalgically inscribed 'fringing the dusty road with harmless gold'. Although this line is taken from an American poem, J. R. Lowell's 'To a Dandelion', Frederick Hurten must surely have been thinking of Stoke where even today dandelions still line some roads in the spring.

After Frederick Hurten's departure for the Avon Pottery, the post of art director at Wardle's seems to have been taken over by his brother Harry. Wardle's were now producing many different tube-lined patterns, some of which were signed by Harry himself (Plate 6). At the same time the company, like Wileman's, was supplying the Regent Street store Liberty's with art wares, though the Wardle backstamp does not appear on these productions. Another new Wardle line, known only from advertisements at present, was described as *pâte-sur-pâte*. Frederick Rhead himself must have been behind this project and no doubt Charlotte and Dollie would again have been responsible for the decorations. A few years later, in 1911, Charlotte herself exhibited some *pâte-sur-pâte* bowls at the Turin International Exhibition.

Meanwhile, Frederick Hurten had moved on from the Avon to another Ohio pottery, the Weller in Zanesville, a thriving centre of the pottery industry and known at the time as Clay City. Unlike the Avon, Weller had already marketed a tube-lined range, *Turada*, though the decorations were merely rather uninspired arabesques. Frederick Hurten introduced his own tubed designs which, characteristically, he named *Rhead Faience*, though these were soon merged with another tubed line with the odd title, *Jap-Birdimal Ware* (Fig 18). These *Jap-Birdimal* designs consisted

Fig 19 Roseville Pottery, teapot from the Dutch creamware range. The same girl appears on a tile tubed by Charlotte Rhead (Fig 26).

of Japanese figures, many of them copied from Japanese prints, as well as animals, fish and birds, the latter for some reason often adorned with large hats, as in the tall vase on left of Fig 18. There seems to have been no precedent for this at Wileman's or Wardle's though geese, similar to those on the small vase in the illustration, did appear on several Wileman designs, as did the bay trees and fish. But the immediate precedent for the tubed fish may have been the Wardle candlestick illustrated in Plate 5, as were the heart-shaped devices, typical of the period, around the neck and foot.

After a year or two, Frederick Hurten moved on again, this time to become the art director of the larger Roseville Pottery, also in Zanesville. The art wares there were the prestige productions while the bread-and-butter lines were the tableware and other useful wares. One popular creamware line that appeared soon after Frederick Hurten's arrival was *Dutch* and, as the name suggests, the printed decorations featured a range of Dutch characters in national dress. Frederick Hurten's father had spent some time in Holland at the end of the nineteenth century and had made many sketches of the local inhabitants. It was on these sketches that most, if not all, of the *Dutch* designs were based. For instance a small girl with a hoop behind her back appeared on many of these *Dutch* tableware designs, including the teapot in Fig 19. She is identical, though with the image reversed, with the girl on a tile tubed by Charlotte Rhead and illustrated in Fig 26, clearly demonstrating the continuing connections between the family on each side of the Atlantic. Moreover the same sketches were used again for an embossed Roseville line, *Holland*. Another of Rhead's productions at Roseville, *Olympic*, tells a similar story. Here the designs were taken, as the name implies, from classical mythology. There were in fact reproductions of works by the eighteenth century artist John Flaxman and provide yet another example of the closeness of the Rhead family and the way members were able to draw on family resources. In 1884 Frederick Alfred Rhead had been awarded as a prize 'for success in the Advanced Section of the Course of Instruction in Art' at the Burslem School of Art, a copy of Flaxman's *Classical Outlines* and it is from this work that most of the *Olympic* designs were taken. Fig 20, for instance, shows an *Olympic* vase depicting 'Juno commanding the Sun to set', an

Fig 20 Roseville Pottery, vase in the Olympic range, 'Juno Commanding the Sun to Set'.

incident from the Trojan War as descibed by Homer in his *Iliad*. Fig 21 shows Flaxman's design for this scene, taken incidentally from Frederick's Rhead's own well-worn copy of the book.

But Frederick Hurten's most prestigious line at Roseville was *Della Robbia*, which he probably named after Harold Rathbone's Arts and Crafts pottery in Birkenhead. These *Della Robbia* pieces were made by

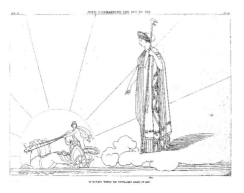

Fig 21 Plate from Frederick Rhead's copy of John Flaxman's 'Classical Outlines'. Frederick Hurten Rhead adapted the designs for the Roseville Olympic range from his father's book (Fig 20).

a process which involved casting in two coloured slips, the design being carved or incised and cut through to the ground colour – a technique which Rhead had learned at Wileman's. The designs were eclectic and feature many of the motifs which Rhead had absorbed in England. The line was evidently profitable too, although it must have been relatively expensive to produce, as it included utilitarian wares such as teapots. Nevertheless, despite these and other successes, in 1908 Frederick Hurten Rhead decided to move on again, this time 'to do some writing on pottery'. But there was still a Rhead presence at Roseville as he arranged for his brother Harry to come from England to take over his job, his Wardle post having virtually collapsed.

For Frederick Alfred Rhead had left Wileman's around 1904 or 1905 and was again working as a freelance designer, supplying patterns to a number of potteries and tile works. This change must have been successful as the family was able to move to a larger house, in Friarswood Road, Newcastle, where Frederick built a kiln in the garden and even had a telephone installed. But one consequence of his new and busy work schedule was that he had to give up his supervision of Wardle's. This turned out to be a disaster for the firm as its business rapidly fell away, so much so that Frederick felt it necessary to remove his daughters Charlotte and Dollie. Two years later Harry left for the United States to take over his brother's post as the Roseville art director.

Frederick now found Charlotte and Dollie work with Keeling & Co. at the Dale Hall Works in Burslem. To their disappointment, Keeling's did not do tube-lining and the girls were employed as enamellers only. The work also involved carrying heavy baskets and boards of ware for long distances within the pottery and the girls soon became disillusioned with the job. So in December 1906 Frederick wrote to William Moorcroft, the distinguished designer and a leading exponent of tube-lining, who had succeeded Frederick Barnard at Macintyre's. Asking whether he had an opening for his daughters, Frederick commented "I cannot think of any other firm where they could be so suitably employed", though rather surprisingly he added, "I regret that they have taken to artistic pursuits".[1] At the time Macintyre's was losing interest in the art pottery side of the business, and although Moorcroft's reply has not survived, it must have been negative. Many years later Charlotte told Mrs. Rose Platt, one of her tube-liners, how disappointed she was at having been turned down for a job with Moorcroft.[2] How long Charlotte and Dollie stayed at Keeling's is not known but they may have moved on to Cauldon Ltd. at Sheldon. Cauldon was the successor to Brown, Westhead, Moore & Co. which, in the nineteenth century, had been one of the most respected manufacturers in the Potteries. In the 1880s its porcelain range had even included some *pâte-sur-pâte*. If indeed the girls did go to Cauldon, they would have been employed only as enamellers.

Fig 22 American Encaustic Tiling Company, Nursery Tile, The Yellow Dwarf, from a series with designs adapted by Frederick Hurten Rhead from children's books by Walter Crane, c1922.

Whatever the case, another change was in the offing. In 1908 Frederick entered into a partnership with a Mr. F. H. Barker to manufacture tiles at the Atlas Tile Works in Vine Street, Hanley and Charlotte and Dollie joined the family business (see Chapter Three). But the enterprise was not a success and by 1910 it had collapsed, bringing great hardship to the Rhead family, most of whose possessions had to be sold to pay the debts incurred. They also had to give up the Newcastle house and return to Porthill where the small semi-detached building they had rented ten years before happened to be empty. Frederick then left to join his sons in the United States, where Harry was having a successful, if not very eventful, career at the Roseville Pottery. Frederick Hurten had meanwhile joined the School of Ceramic Art at University City, on the outskirts of St Louis, as instructor in pottery. This School, part of an ambitious educational project set up by the entrepreneur Edward G. Lewis for the American Womans League, was headed by the French ceramist and *pâte-sur-pâte* artist Taxile Doat. For a time Frederick Alfred also hoped to get a job there but this came to nothing and as he could not settle down in America, he soon returned to England. As it turned out, this was fortunate as the University City project collapsed soon after. Frederick Hurten then left for California, working first for a mission in Arequipa near San Francisco where he trained girls recovering from tuberculosis in pottery techniques. He then went on to set up his own pottery in Santa Barbara. But the constraints imposed by World War One proved too great and when that enterprise also failed, he returned to Zanesville.

There he obtained the post of research director at the American Encaustic Tiling Company, claimed at the time to be the largest tile-making concern in the world. Although his work there was largely concerned with architectural projects, he also set up an Arts & Crafts Division for the production of art pottery, much of which was sold through the company's New York office. Productions even included some *pâte-sur-pâte*, worked by his second wife Loiz, he and Agnes having parted company in California.

Fig 23 Mosaic Tile Company, Tile Ye Good King Arthur, from 'The Baby's Own Opera' by Walter Crane. Perhaps adapted by Harry Rhead in response to his brother's Crane tiles for the rival American Encaustic Tiling Company.

A series of children's tiles also appeared with designs copied from Walter Crane's *The Baby's Opera* and other children's books (Fig 22). Ten years later he was offered a professorship at the Ohio State University but turned it down, electing instead to become art director of another large company, the Homer Laughlin China Company of Newell, West Virginia. There he remained until his death in 1942, creating among other lines, the colourful 'mix and match' *Fiesta* range of tableware which he claimed as 'the most successful table ware line in any factory anywhere . . .'.[3] The original *Fiesta* ware, which included a tomato red colour made with radio-active uranium glaze, is now very collectable. *Fiesta* is still made today, keeping Frederick Hurten's name as its designer alive, though his red uranium glaze has long since been discontinued.

Harry stayed on as art director of the Roseville Pottery for a dozen years or so when he left to become manager of the faience department of the Mosaic Tile Company, also in Zanesville. There he was perhaps responsible for the appearance of another set of Crane tiles (Fig 23), rivals to his brother's productions at American Encaustic. Then in 1923 he helped to establish a new firm there, the Standard Tile Company. At first successful, it fell on hard times during the recession of the 1930s and finally closed during World War Two. Harry died in Florida in 1950.

While their father was in America, Charlotte and Dollie were left to fend for themselves. Charlotte obtained a job with the tile manufacturer T. & R. Boote[4] perhaps as a designer. She may also have worked for Marsden's, and possibly some other companies too. As for Dollie, she had long planned to become a nurse, but had been unable to start training as she was under age. In her early twenties, and with the help of a friend, she obtained a place at Addenbrooks Hospital in Cambridge, where she qualified as a midwife, a profession she subsequently followed with success. She retained her tube-lining skills too and is remembered for having taken Charlotte's place very competently at Burgess & Leigh in the late 1920s when her sister was on holiday.[5]

When Frederick returned from America, he and Charlotte seem to have worked for a time with the firm of Birks, Rawlins at the Vine Pottery in Stoke-on-Trent. Frederick's close friend, Lawrence Birks, the Managing Director, had been a fellow apprentice of Louis Solon at Minton's in the 1870s, and he too was a skilled exponent of the *pâte-sur-pâte* decorative technique. With Frederick's and Charlotte's contributions to the display, the Birks, Rawlins exhibit at the Turin International Exhibition in 1911 attracted a great deal of favourable attention and the company was awarded a diploma of honour. The exhibits included a pair of bowls, *Ships*, in *pâte-sur-pâte* by Charlotte as well as a series of tube-lined vases by Charlotte and Dollie. These were of special interest as they were tubed on porcelain instead of the usual earthenware.

Early in 1912 Frederick Rhead was appointed art director of Wood & Sons in Burslem where he was, according to some accounts, joined by Charlotte. Their work for Wood's and its associated companies, Bursley Ltd. and the Ellgreave Pottery Co., is described in Chapter Four though Charlotte may possibly have spent some of this time with A. G. Richardson. She later moved on to Burgess & Leigh and then in 1932 to A. G. Richardson, makers of *Crown Ducal Ware*, finally returning to another Wood company, H. J. Wood, early in World War Two. These last stages of Charlotte's career and her death in November 1947 are also described in subsequent chapters.

If information about Charlotte's professional career is patchy, details of her private life are even scantier. As a successful designer, her work was widely publicised yet the person behind the reputation preferred to remain out of the limelight. So elusive was she, even to those who worked closely with her, that it is difficult to evaluate the personality which shaped so distinguished a career. People who knew Charlotte tend to fall back on short generalised remarks which evoke her physical characteristics. She is variously described as 'petite', 'prematurely grey', 'white haired' with 'large dark eyes', as 'a dog lover' and with the generalisation that she was 'a lovely lady'. Charlotte so seldom spoke about herself that her colleagues rarely got beneath the surface of the outward manner. One of the main reasons must have been her extreme shyness and old-fashioned reserve. She disliked any form of violence. Once, at a dance she was attending, a fight broke out and she asked to be taken home immediately. But if she was a quiet woman, she was one of strong principles. She never swore, and the uttering of an involuntary 'damn' by one of the girls could result in being sent home at once – with a consequent loss of wages. On the other hand she would always fight for the welfare of 'her girls', especially the tube-liners whom she regarded as the decorators with the greatest skills, and she made sure, even when she was dying, that their pay was fixed at the highest possible rate. More than once she advised a girl who wanted to buy a faulty piece – a 'second' – to allow it to get dirty so as to secure it for the lowest possible price.

The people who worked for Charlotte speak of her as a kind person who always attracted great personal affection and loyalty. Technically she excelled at her craft and always insisted on the highest standards – everything had to be 'just right'. She had the experience to ensure that everything was just right, too, for her background and training had given her a profound knowledge of all aspects of commercial potting. She knew that it was her job to design products that would sell, and sell at the right price, so she was very cost-conscious and was always on the lookout for ways of reducing costs without lowering quality.

In spite of the success of her designs, particularly those produced for Richardson's in the 1930s, she was not well known in her lifetime. The trade press often commented on this fact and as late as 1937 a reporter, interviewing Charlotte, observed that some women designers were known to a wide public while one or two others were 'hiding their light under a bushel'. He clearly had difficulty with the interview for he went on to remark 'that owing to Miss Rhead's extremely shy disposition, she was rather reticent to say anything about herself'. Indeed more emerged from the interview about other members of the Rhead family than about Charlotte herself. The reporter nevertheless concluded: 'In real pottery production, science and art must go together, and Miss Rhead has had the most happy knack of retaining the essential virtue of sincerity in the matter of technical knowledge and creative sense'. And, with reference to tube-lining, he added 'Miss Rhead has "individualised" it, putting it in a class of its own; in fact it can be said with truth that her designs express her own personality'.[6] Perhaps Charlotte had worked too long in the shadow of her father for her to overcome her social diffidence and to 'sell herself', or perhaps the traumas of her early illnesses and of her late and defective education remained.

How is she to be assessed today as a designer? In her lifetime she certainly earned the respect of her peers and of those who worked under her direction. She also attracted imitators. A number of potteries marketed tube-lined wares in the 1930s, among them Royal Cauldon. Edith Gaiter, Cauldon's designer, was undoubtedly influenced by Charlotte's work; her falling leaf pattern, *Autumn Leaves* (Plate 83), for instance was surely inspired by – if not actually copied from – Charlotte's *Golden Leaves* (Plate 72).

The best known female commercial designers of the 1930s were Susie Cooper and Clarice Cliff. Charlotte certainly lacked both Miss Cooper's commercial acumen and Clarice Cliff's flamboyant temperament and flair for publicity. Charlotte was not a particularly original designer nor was she a 'modernist', although her work does reflect the changing decorative styles of her day. The derivation of few of her designs is directly traceable and it is clear that her patterns were adapted from many different historical and contemporary sources and, above all, her own close observation of plant forms. Indeed the majority of her designs are based on plant forms, a predilection which may have been fostered by the many books on the subject of design which appeared around the turn of the century, most notably perhaps Lewis F. Day's *Nature in Ornament. Modern Practical Design*, published a few years later by her uncle George Woolliscroft Rhead, must also have had a strong influence on her ideas. In a long introductory section devoted to the subject of plant form as the basis of ornament, George Woolliscroft explained:

'I shall endeavour to show, therefore, in the following pages, that with a sufficiently careful selection, ornament, the finest ornament, already exists in Nature, and that the different conventions adopted in ornamental art at various periods are mainly in the direction of simplification, and were necessitated by the exigencies of the method employed and the limitations of the material.'[7]

Charlotte would doubtless also have been influenced by her father's view that the most original British pottery designer was Thomas Toft and that Josiah Wedgwood had done the country a disservice by 'switching the Staffordshire potters off the track of originality, and made them copyists of the Greeks'.[8] As Frederick frankly admitted soon after, 'We Englishmen are more imitative than creative'.[9]

Charlotte's virtue was that she could take several ideas and, aiming at a composition that was strong in its own right, unite them into a coherent whole. She was particularly successful when the decoration was to be tube-lined and in this respect she had few equals. Clarice Cliff does not appear to have attempted to use this technique, and Susie Cooper only did so to a very limited extent, even employing Charlotte's tube-liners who would occasionally 'moonlight' for her. Cooper's tube-lined designs are not very significant and she probably realised that her strengths lay elsewhere for she did not persist with this technique. As for Charlotte, having produced a design, she would adapt and modify it for application to many different shapes, and in this she excelled. Commercially the results were immensely popular and this, after all, is one of the most important tests of a successful designer. Judged on these terms, *The Pottery Gazette* was right when, on her death, it claimed that the pottery industry 'had lost one of its most talented designers'.[10]

CHAPTER THREE

The Rheads as Tile Designers and Decorators

Frederick Rhead's involvement with the manufacture and decoration of tiles seems to have developed early in his career, stimulated perhaps by his old master at Minton's, the *pâte-sur-pâte* artist Louis Solon. In 1878 Solon had designed a famous series of fireplace surround tiles; executed in sgraffito, they were emblematic of the ten leading potting nations of the world, and were shown that year at the Paris International Exhibition. In 1903 one of Rhead's own fireplace designs, *Faust and the Fire Maiden*, was illustrated in *The Studio* magazine. Interestingly the same design reappeared a few months later in the American Arts and Crafts journal *Keramic Studio*.

From the 1880s onwards Frederick Rhead had provided designs for several tile manufacturers, among them the Crystal Porcelain Tile Co.[1] and Sherwin & Cotton, both

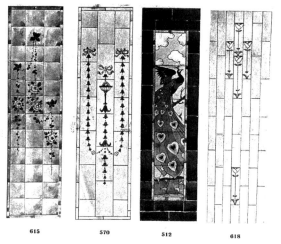

615   570   512   618

Fig 24 Page from a Barker, Rhead catalogue of printed designs, c1909.

of Hanley. In view of his interest in tube-lining, it is no surprise to find that it was he who devised a method of applying the technique to dust-pressed tiles. In the course of a long series of articles entitled *Tiles Historic Modern*,[2] published between 1922 and 1924, he wrote: 'The first attempts to apply "tube lining" to tiles were made on the unfired dust tile, but this was not found practicable on account of the fragile nature of the dust tiles, and also because the surface of the tile was too soft for the passage of the glass quill. The present writer experimented on biscuit tiles, and succeeded in making a slip that would not contract or shell off'.[3] He repeated this claim again in 1924[4], adding that the process, which must have been introduced around 1900, had been developed in conjunction with Léon Solon.

Léon, the eldest son of Louis Solon, was the art director of Minton's at that time and also a prominent member of the Art Worker's Guild. His interest in applying tube-lining to tiles is evident not only from the *Secessionist Ware* range which he was developing for Minton's, but also from the tile panels he designed and decorated himself, many of which were shown at the several Arts and Crafts and International Exhibitions of the era. Frederick Rhead, too, had good personal reasons for developing this technique though neither Wardle's, over whose output he held a watching brief, nor Wileman's, where he was art director, were tile makers; the few tiles which were included in Wileman's Intarsio range had printed and not tubed decorations. So, beside his main commitments, he was evidently supplying designs to tile manufacturers as well. Among them may have been the Henry Richards Tile Co., noted for its range of tiles with tube-lined Art Nouveau decorations. Some of this firm's productions have motifs similar to those used by Frederick Rhead on the tube-lined *Elers* and *Trellis* patterns which he designed for Wood's in 1913 (Plates 7 and 9). Not too much can be deduced from this as Frederick himself had borrowed several of Charles Rennie Mackintosh's fashionable motifs for his designs.

Fig 25 Tile tube-lined by Charlotte Rhead. Castle scene. Value £800/$1640.

According to Frederick's daughter, Katherine Rhead, he was also designing tiles for Lottie and Dollie to tube-line at this time. These seem to have been intended mainly as decorative items for family and friends,[5] although some may have also been made for sale. There is no contemporary evidence on this point but it seems quite likely, as the enterprising Rheads were always on the lookout for new sources of income.

In 1908 Frederick Rhead embarked on the manufacture of tiles, and in partnership with F. H. Barker, purchased the Atlas Tile Works, Vine Street, Hanley from a German, Francis Theimeicke. A surviving Barker, Rhead catalogue (Fig 24) suggests that the standard products of the firm had printed decorations. Majolica and tube-lined tiles were also produced, and the only productions of the company which have so far been positively identified are tubed. These are mounted in oak frames stamped *Barker, Rhead* on their backs, suggesting that the company sold them as ornaments – a continuation of the practice which Frederick had started a few years earlier. As before, these tubed tiles must have been decorated by Charlotte or Dollie Rhead.

Other decorated tube-lined tiles, some in similar but unstamped oak frames, presumably belong to the earlier period already described. Although no signed examples have come to light, a number belong to friends or relatives of the Rhead family and are invariably assigned to Charlotte by tradition. Other similar tiles occasionally come on the market, and these can be attributed to Charlotte or Dollie on stylistic grounds. Several related tiles were also found in an outbuilding, after Dollie's death in 1981, at the house in Watlands Avenue, Wolstanton, which she had inherited from Charlotte.

The tubed tile designs fall into a number of distinct thematic groups:

1 Castles and landscapes
2 Dutch scenes
3 Female heads in profile
4 Animals
5 Figures in archaic or period dress
6 Ships and galleons
7 Nursery Rhymes

According to Katherine Rhead[6] some of the designs were provided by her father, Frederick Rhead, and the probability is that he was responsible for most of them. A few may have been Charlotte's, among them perhaps an illustration of Jack and Jill climbing the hill to fetch a pail of water. One scene, an urban landscape, depicts Penkhull Square in Stoke where Lawrence Birks and his family at one time lived. He was a close friend of Frederick's, and, like him, had been apprenticed to Louis Solon at Minton's in the 1870s. So this design may even have been supplied by him. But the castles (Fig 25) and landscapes generally, which seem to be reasonably

Fig 26 Tile tube-lined by Charlotte Rhead. The Dutch girl was adapted from a drawing by Frederick Rhead. Value £750/$1350

Fig 27 Tile tube-lined by Charlotte Rhead. Female head. One of a series, based on the same model. Value £600/$1080.

Fig 28 Tile tube-lined by Charlotte Rhead. Perhaps a portrait of the family dog. Value £750/$1535.

accurate typographical represen-tations and perhaps drawn on the spot, are likely to have been the work of Frederick.

The Dutch scenes appear to have been adapted from sketches made by Frederick Rhead during a visit he made to the Netherlands at the end of the nineteenth century. One such is the tubed Dutch girl illustrated in Fig 26. The same design also appeared a few years later on a printed tableware range named *Dutch*, a product of the Roseville Pottery in Zanesville, Ohio. At the time Frederick H Rhead was the art director there, confirming that the members of the Rhead family maintained close contacts despite being separated by the Atlantic ocean.

Fig 29 Tube-lined tile depicting a couple in traditional dress. Value £1250/$2250.

The stylised female heads clearly derive from the same profile turned either to the right or the left. They appear in several versions wearing different headdresses against landscapes or interior settings (fig. 27 and plate 4). Animals, on the other hand, are relatively uncommon (fig. 28). A small tile depicting a dog is likely to be modelled on a family pet, a fox terrier curiously named Tax.[7] The figures in archaic or mediaeval dress (fig. 29 and plate 4) may have been copied from books, or perhaps adapted by Frederick himself from these sources. When tubed tiles are always worth acquiring.

Among the illustrations in the Barker, Rhead catalogue is a printed tile depicting a galleon under sail (fig. 30). The same vessel appears again on one of the framed tube-lined Barker, Rhead tiles and a larger tubed version (fig. 31), although unmarked, can presumably also be attributed to the company. But the Barker, Rhead enterprise had a very short life and by 1910 it had failed, bankrupting Frederick and causing great hardship to the Rhead family.[8] It is probably for this reason that so little is known about its productions.

Some tiles with tube-lined decorations, and evidently the work of one of the Rheads, carry the marks

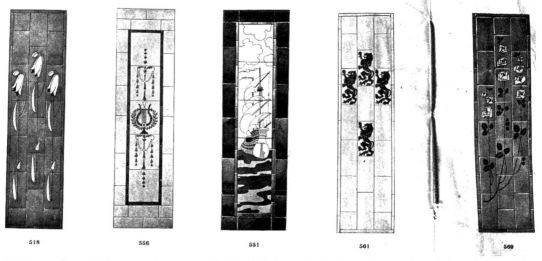

518   556   551   561   569

Fig 30 Page from a Barker, Rhead catalogue of printed designs, c1909. A tube-lined version of the galleon was also made (Fig 31).

of other manufacturers, T. A. Simpson (Cliff Bank Works, Tunstall) and George Woolliscroft & Sons being among them. Presumably these were purchased as blanks, and after Charlotte or Dollie had decorated them, perhaps at home, were fired elsewhere. Many of these productions must predate the ill-fated Barker, Rhead enterprise[9] though it is reasonable to assume that some were made after the closure of the firm when Charlotte was working for another tile manufacturer, either T.&R. Boote or the Marsden Tile Co. Although information about her work at this time is extremely sketchy, it does seem likely that she continued to be involved with tile production in one capacity or another until she joined Wood & Sons (see Chapter Four).

Fig 31 Tile with tube-lined decoration by Charlotte Rhead. Perhaps a product of the Barker, Rhead company (see Fig 30). Value £750/$1535.

CHAPTER FOUR

Wood & Sons Bursley Ltd.
The Ellgreave Pottery Co.

Frederick Rhead, Charlotte's father, had been without a job since Barker, Rhead, the tile firm which he managed, collapsed around 1910 leaving him bankrupt. Joining his sons Frederick Hurten and Harry in the United States, there appeared to be a possibility of his obtaining employment at the Art Academy of the the Peoples University, in University City, a suburb of Saint Louis in Missouri. At the time Frederick Hurten was the pottery instructor in the Academy's ceramics division, which was headed by the Frenchman Taxile Doat. Doat had recently been retired by the Director of the National Porcelain Manufactory at Sèvres where he had been the leading *pâte-sur-pâte* decorator. The prospect of working for Doat must have been very attractive to Frederick, but nothing came of it, mainly on account of opposition by another Frenchman, Emile Diffloth, Doat's chemist. As it turned out this was just as well, for the Peoples University collapsed soon after. By that time Frederick had already returned to England and, after a few months working with his old friend Lawrence Birks at the Birks, Rawlins Pottery in Stoke, he was engaged early in 1912 as the art director for Wood & Sons.[1]

When Frederick joined Wood's, the company was under the energetic management of Harry Wood, and operated at two potteries in Burslem, the Trent and the New Wharf, where Frederick set up his office. The main productions were dinner, tea, toilet, hotel and badged wares and what were termed 'high-class and general fancies'. A third pottery in Burslem, the Stanley, was run in conjunction with the Trent and New Wharf Potteries by one of Harry's brothers, while a fourth, the Alexandra Pottery, was managed by other members of the family as a separate company, H. J. Wood Ltd.

Frederick's first responsibility as art director was designing the main bread-and-butter lines, but all his training and instincts must have made led him to expand the production of the art ware, the 'fancies'. High on his agenda was a tube-lined range, a technique hitherto untried at Wood's, and soon after his arrival two such lines appeared. These were *Elers* (Plates 9 and 119) and *Trellis* (Plate 7) which must have found buyers almost immediately as they can still be found in some quantity. Both patterns incorporate several of Charles Rennie Mackintosh's Art Nouveau motifs, as does the simpler tube-lined *Check* which Frederick may have designed soon afterwards (Fig 32). But unlike *Elers* and *Trellis*, *Check* is rarely found today, so production may have been limited.

Another of Frederick's long-held ambition was to market a commercial *pâte-sur-pâte* series. He had attempted to do so both at Wileman's and Wardle's though with indifferent success. Now he tried again, this time with gratifying results. In 1913 Wood's issued a special catalogue, *Pâte-sur-Pâte – A Notable Revival*, illustrating a dozen different patterns which, it was stated, were 'only intended as examples'. Wood's sought to reassure buyers who might have been put off by the high cost of *pâte-sur-pâte* wares by adding that these were being put on the market 'at prices well within the reach of the average man', the decorations being 'executed entirely by hand by a staff of trained artists under the direction of Mr. Rhead. Every piece is signed by Mr. Rhead, a guarantee of perfect execution and careful and artistic production generally . . . '. In fact, despite the name, these commercial *pâte-sur-pâte* wares seem to have been largely another, though more elaborate, tube-lined range (Plates 8 and 121). Even so they must have proved popular, since production continued for more than a decade. The successes of both the tube-lined wares and the *pâte-sur-pâte* lines no doubt convinced Harry Wood of the desirability of including them as a regular part of Wood's output.

Charlotte Rhead appears to have joined Wood's soon after her father. When he was in America she had probably been working for the tile

Fig 32 Wood & Sons tube-lined vase, Check pattern. Value £275/$535.

manufacturers T. & R. Boote and Marsden's.[2] Although her role with these companies is not known, it is likely to have been mainly designing and decorating the tiles which were so popular at the time for butchers' and other high-street shops. By this time she was certainly an established designer and a highly skilled tube-liner who specialised in this type of decoration. Her job at Wood's was presumably to train and supervise the tube-liners who were needed for the new productions and to provide some designs herself. She must have been involved with the *pâte-sur-pâte* productions too, as a supervisor and sometimes as a designer. A *pâte-sur-pâte* pattern of stylised three-pointed leaves, which was not illustrated in the Wood's catalogue and not marked with the usual Frederick Rhead facsimile signature, has very similar features to one of her tube-lined designs, Bursley pattern no. 439. She was certainly proficient in this difficult technique and had exhibited a pair of *pâte-sur-pâte* bowls with the title *Ships* at the Turin International Exhibition in 1911.[3]

Fig 33 Wood & Sons, plaque tube-lined by Charlotte Rhead, depicting a Japanese girl playing a shamisen with printed Prunus pattern border, c1916. Value £1200/$2340.

In addition to designing, Charlotte tubed some patterns herself, including a pair of elaborate and uncommon plaques, one decorated with a Japanese girl playing a *shamisen* (Fig 33) and the other with a seated Japanese female figure holding a letter in her left hand (Fig 34). These were probably made during World War One, and are found either with with a standard *Prunus* border, introduced by Frederick Rhead as a straightforward pattern for the decoration of bowls and other useful wares, or with a plain blue border. They also appear in various colour arrangements and, unaccountably, are often unmarked. Around 1927 the image of the seated figure with the letter appeared again in reverse as Burgess & Leigh pattern no. 4011.

For other tube-lined patterns Charlotte would also have made the pounces,[4] or pricked patterns, which the tube-liners needed in order to apply the decorations to the varied Wood shapes. These shapes were mainly bowls, vases, bottles and ornamental items, some derived from Greek or Middle Eastern forms for which her

Fig 34 Wood & Sons, plaque tube-lined by Charlotte Rhead, pair to Fig 33. Plain blue border. Value £1200/$2340.

father was at least partly responsible. The *Elers* and *Trellis* patterns were also applied to trinket sets – regarded as an essential accessory by many women at the time – and to the equally essential toilet sets. But Charlotte did not confine herself to designing these more expensive items, and some of Wood's printed patterns must have been her work too. A good example is *Arras* which, to judge by its name, must have made its appearance on the market around 1917. Some of its motifs, pomegranates and flowers, reappear later on her popular tube-lined patterns, such as *Pomona* (Plate 12).

Another Wood's tube-lined design which can be attributed to Charlotte on stylistic grounds is *Persian* (Plate 10) which perhaps dates from about 1918. Soon after this Wood's began to market these productions under the name *Bursley Ware*, 'Bursley' being adopted from the fictional name Arnold Bennett gave Burslem in his novels about the 'Five Towns'. The *Bursley Ware* range attracted the attention of the trade press at the British Industries Fair in 1919. *The Pottery and Glass Record* referred in its March issue to a bowl with 'conventionalised bird motif with combination blue and green on old gold ground', and to another exhibit with 'conventional peony and other floral effects in harmonious glazes'.[5] The bird motif pattern remains unidentified, but the 'conventional peony' was probably the *Rhodian* design which featured a band of large red flowers, with spiky petals and yellow centres on green stems, and blue pointed leaves. *The Pottery Gazette* reporter at the Fair also seems to have been impressed, succinctly describing the *Rhodian* ware as 'powerful'.[6] Another design in the Bursley Ware range which may have been exhibited at the Fair was *Seed Poppy* (Plate 11), a colourful and popular pattern that remained in production for a decade or so. *Seed Poppy* is sometimes mistaken for Moorcroft's *Pomegranate*, also featuring large circular tube-lined seeds, and with which it was no doubt intended to compete. *Rhodian* ware also bears a strong family resemblance to George Cartlidge's successful tube-lined *Morrisware* range which he was designing at the time for the firm of Sampson Hancock. A list of all the known Wood & Sons tube-lined designs follows this chapter.

While Charlotte was working on her tube-lined and other designs, Frederick was mainly concerned with the production of the basic 'bread-and-butter' output, most notably the tableware, of which his best known, and certainly most enduring, design was *Yuan* (Plate 13). Introduced in 1916, it was still in production until recently. This book does not aim to cover the tablewares of the period, which are of limited interest to many collectors. However a number of these designs were adapted as ornamental wares (Plate 15), and as these are collectible, a list of them, with a description of the main patterns, also follows later in this chapter.

Wood's art wares continued to sell well and in 1920 Frederick Rhead persuaded Harry Wood to increase production by acquiring the Crown Pottery, a building conveniently situated near the Stanley Pottery. At the same time a new company, Bursley Ltd.,[7] was set up to operate the pottery and Frederick Rhead moved his office there from the New Wharf. The Crown was well equipped and had an innovatory Dressler Tunnel Oven, the first to be installed in the Potteries. Key staff were also transferred from other Wood potteries

Fig 35 The tube-liner Katie Wall and the paintresses Nellie Caton and Cissie Breton outside the Crown Pottery in Burslem, c1922.

as was Charlotte, who moved, along with four tube-liners, into an office next to her father (Fig 35). The Crown now became the centre for the manufacture of the Wood art wares although its 'bread-and-butter' lines continued to be the still essential toilet wares – jugs, basins, chamber pots and other necessaries. To cater for a more affluent customer, and combining a measure of art with utility, some of these toilet wares were tube-lined.

In 1921 Wood's made another acquisition in Burslem, taking over a bankrupt works there and renaming it the Ellgreave Pottery.[8] This factory specialised in red-bodied wares, mainly teapots, though some tableware and fancies, such as vases, were also made, using, it is said, the same seam of red clay that the Elers Brothers had first exploited around 1700. In 1923 or thereabouts Charlotte seems to have been given the task of making the rather plain Ellgreave wares more attractive. A new range, *Lottie Rhead Ware*, was introduced. It was decorated with a trellis pattern, the lattices of which, thickly tubed in white and blue or brown, and sometimes straight and sometimes undulating, were applied to the red-bodied dinner and tea ware (Plate 17). Each piece was marked with a special *Lottie Rhead Ware* backstamp, the first time that her name had been formally linked to her commercial designs. This rather coarsely decorated ware is found with both dark and light brown grounds. Today it is relatively uncommon and may not have been a great success as the red body is very susceptible to chipping, and much of it must have been broken and thrown away. Charlotte may also have been responsible for a number of vases and bowls decorated underglaze with floral designs. These are usually marked with an Ellgreave backstamp and a stylised image taken from an element in the decoration, a device which Frederick had introduced at Wood's, and which he also adopted for a few Bursley Ltd. productions which were not given pattern numbers. One example, for the popular *Amstel* pattern, is illustrated with other backstamps at the end of this chapter.

Charlotte's work for the Ellgreave Pottery was doubtless something of a sideline as her main involvement was with Bursley Ltd. at the Crown Pottery. Unfortunately the Bursley pattern books for the 1920s have not survived. Her designs were not base marked as they were at the Ellgreave Pottery or, a few years later, at Burgess & Leigh. So deductions about her designs have to be made based on stylistic considerations, press reports and the memories of people who worked with her. As her father continued to design art wares for Bursley Ltd., as well as the basic lines for all the Wood's potteries, it is not always easy to decide who did what. Doubtless, too, there were some designs to which both father and daughter contributed. There were also assistant designers, Horace Wain, Jack Gryce and, at the end of the decade, Jack Butler, but comparatively little individual work by them is readily identifiable. Latterly Frederick tended to make use of underglaze prints, but he was responsible for more elaborate pieces too, including some with tube-lined decoration. As the company productions from this decade are now very collectible, the list that follows includes all known Bursley Ltd. patterns up to around 1931. Charlotte herself was undoubtedly responsible for most of the tube-lined designs with fruit or floral decoration which appeared up to the end of 1926, and even for many after that, while Frederick and the assistant designers probably provided the remainder.

At the important International Exhibition of Modern Decorative and Industrial Arts held in Paris in 1925, Wood's was one of the relatively few English potteries to exhibit. Productions of both Wood & Sons and Bursley Ltd. were included in the company display, the official catalogue describing the Bursley ware as:

Toilet Ware and every variety of decorated 'fancies'. These are mostly decorated by hand, and comprise underglaze decorations, matt glazes, lustres and decorations in coloured pastes. The Arabian and Persian matt glazes and Italian yellow and blue lustres may be specially noted as well as the fruit decoration in suave blues and greens.[9]

This contemporary description gives a good idea of the great variety of Bursley decorations at this time, many of which can be recognised in the following patterns – for example, the Arabian matt glaze on patterns 471, 648 and 649 (Plate 22) and the Italian yellow and blue lustres on the 'Dragon' coffee-pot, pattern 411, (Plate 21). The Department of Overseas Trade official report on the pottery at the Exhibition was written by Gordon Forsyth,[10] a critic who held strong views on pottery design. He observed that Wood's 'showed excellent examples of their work'.[11] Nevertheless the company only received the rather lowly award of a 'Mention' for its display, which must have been something of a disappointment both to Harry Wood and to Frederick Rhead.

Charlotte left Wood's towards the end of 1926 when she moved down the road to another Burslem firm, Burgess & Leigh (see Chapter Five). Frederick remained at Wood's for a further three years, and after his departure both he and Charlotte kept in touch with Harry Wood. So it is not surprising to find that several of Charlotte's designs continued to be produced by Wood's for some years after her departure. She had probably made a number, perhaps most, of these before she left; designers as prolific as the Rheads would have been responsible for far more patterns than could possibly have gone into production at any one time. Even so, it seems likely that Charlotte went on supplying Wood's with some designs after her departure, at first no doubt through her father as she lived with her parents. Some of these patterns are unsatisfactory, among them a series of tube-lined plaques which appeared in the late 1920s. Apparently designed by Charlotte, they are overlaid by panels painted with oriental style designs, the work of Horace Wain. It is hard to imagine Charlotte at all pleased with this development. However, evidence that she did produce late work for Wood's comes from a tube-lined plaque still in the possession of a member of the Rhead family. By tradition this plaque was made by Charlotte and stylistically it certainly appears to be her work, but it has the pattern number 1952, which indicates that it was made around 1931.

It is not known precisely why Charlotte decided to move to Burgess & Leigh in 1926, though no doubt there were several contributory factors. The General Strike that year curtailed production and the shortage of coal eventually forced the Crown Pottery to close. At the same time her father had a serious operation which may have disrupted her work and even brought her into conflict with other designers. She was used to working under the direction of her father with whom she got on well, and she may have found it less easy to take orders from others. The last straw could have been a fire which broke out at the Crown Pottery in August just as work was about to restart. This did serious damage to the machinery in the jigger shops and engine house, and destroyed many of the moulds, making some thirty employees 'idle for an indefinite period'.[12] Then again, Charlotte, having perhaps been offered more money by Burgess & Leigh, may have been glad to have the opportunity to establish herself as an independent designer. Although she was evidently happy

Fig 36 Wood & Sons, vases designed by Frederick Rhead, Korea (value £600/$1170 pair) and Elers (value £800/$1560 pair) patterns.

living with her parents, her father was a powerful personality, a senior and much respected art director, and the founder and President of the Pottery Managers' and Officials' Association. As she had turned forty, it is reasonable to assume that she would have welcomed her independence. In the event the move was an important step along her career path as a skilled designer and all-round potter.

Notes for Collectors

Most of the Wood & Sons, Bursley Ltd. and Ellgreave Pottery productions carry printed backstamps on their bases. The Wood pieces usually have the pattern name together with a stylised image taken from a portion of the decoration, and the imprint 'Wood & Sons'. Many of these will probably have been designed before the name Bursley Ware was introduced around the end of 1919. There were at least four main Bursley Ware backstamps and these are illustrated at the end of this chapter. Exceptionally, some of the designs which originated at Wood's and were subsequently transferred to Bursley Ltd., retain their old style backstamp with 'Bursley Ware' substituted for 'Wood & Sons' while the popular *Seed Poppy* pattern may appear with both 'Wood's' and 'Bursley Ware' marks. *Seed Poppy* was later given a pattern number, P28. The Ellgreave *Lottie Rhead Ware* mark was discussed in the previous section.

Other marks which may appear on the bases of Bursley Ltd. productions are a three- or four-figure pattern number (*Seed Poppy* and a few others are unusual in having only two digits – see above). There may also be a tube-liner's mark and a decorator's mark, the latter invariably painted. It has only been possible in very few cases to correlate these marks with the names of the women employed at the time, though a list showing some of the known tube-liners follows. Collectors should note that although Frederick Rhead's name appears on some of his designs, *Elers* and the *pâte-sur-pâte* range among them, none of Charlotte's designs for Wood's or Bursley Ltd. were marked with her name.[13] If it does appear, it is likely to be a fraudulent recent addition.

Although pattern numbers were used at the Crown Pottery, the old system of marking some pieces with a pattern name and stylised device only was also retained, mainly for a small number of Frederick Rhead's underglaze designs. These are listed below.

There are many references to Charlotte's designs in the contemporary trade press, but she seems never to have been mentioned by name. Moreover all these references apply to her earlier patterns which have two- or three-figure numbers and it can be deduced that at the time she left in 1926, patterns with numbers around 900 were being used. By comparison, none of the patterns with four-figure numbers can be identified as hers from contemporary reports though there can be no doubt that she was responsible for some of them. They can be attributed to her not only on stylistic grounds and on the evidence of one of the tube-liners,[14] but also from the tube-lined plaque with pattern number 1952. As described in the previous section, this plaque is still in the possession of a member of the Rhead family and is by tradition firmly attributed to Charlotte Rhead. A surviving Wood's Mixing Department record book indicated that patterns with numbers around 1900 were being produced about 1930.

Towards the end of the 1920s a number of plaques were produced by Bursley Ltd. consisting of tube-lined designs overlaid with panels decorated with oriental motifs. The tube-lined designs would appear to be Charlotte's, but the panels were the work of another designer, Horace Wain. Examples seen have the Bursley backstamp no. 10 and include pattern numbers 1325, 1326, 1327 and 1419. These 'oriental' plaques often carry an additional mark, 'Lawley's', and were evidently intended to be sold through the Lawley's chain of shops. They may date from 1929 and be the 'handsome and refined pieces in Japanese designs in solid colours decorated in raised paste by celebrated artists' to which a contemporary report in the trade press referred.[15]

It should also be noted that the Wood companies sometimes produced wares specifically for certain shops or retailers, among them Woolworth's and Hales, Hancock & Godwin. Such wares were marked with the name of the retailer, while Hales, Hancock & Godwin had a special backstamp depicting a Toby Jug and the initials H H & G LTD (no. 12).

Another special backstamp of Wood's in the 1920s was applied to an unusual shaped pot named the 'Cosy'.[16] The shape had been patented in 1921 by its designer, Edmund William Abram, who described it at the time as 'the perfect teapot' though to increase its potential sale he also called it a coffee pot. The following May he registered the name 'Cosy' as a trademark. Earthenware 'Cosy' pots were originally made by several manufacturers, among them Booth's and Pountney's of Bristol, though Wood's had the largest share of the market. When Abram's company, Abram Allware, went into liquidation around 1926,

Wood's inherited the patents for the pot which it continued to make until about 1932. It was produced in a large number of decorative finishes, including Frederick Rhead's *Trellis* (Plate 7), and Charlotte Rhead's *Seed Poppy* (Plate 11) and Bursley pattern no. 726 (Plate 13). The same illustration shows a 'Cosy' with one of Frederick's printed patterns, *Yuan*. A typical 'Cosy' backstamp is illustrated along with others at the end of this chapter (no. 6).

Wood & Sons and Bursley Ltd. Decorators
Tube-liners and their marks
A Annie Castle?
B
D
K Katie Wall
N Nellie Morris
S
W Winnie Wall
y
29
.3. This resembles a mark used by one of the Burgess & Leigh tube-liners, probably Mary Jackson or Hilda Machin (see Chapter Five).

Wood & Sons Printed Patterns for Ornamental Wares.
The following designs can be attributed to Frederick Rhead, or where indicated, Charlotte Rhead.

Brocade	Overall small blue flower design with large coloured peony flowers and seed heads. Made for Woolworth's.
Caliph	Blue peony flowers backed by a network of interconnecting flower-stems.
Chung	Large stylised flower-heads in shades of blue with pointed and scrolling petals amid conventional Chinese motifs; white ground. The pattern was also made with a red ground.
Formosa	Bird in flight amid pink and orange peony flower-heads on stems; made with white and black grounds.
Kang-Hi	Watery and rocky Chinese landscape against a background of houses on stilts. Made in plain blue and coloured versions (Plate 15).
Korea	Exotic bird in white and gold with scaly body and large tail, smaller flying bird and foliage; black ground. Also made in a coloured version on a black ground (Fig 36).
Kylin	Blue dragon design in panel amid cloud scrolls and other Chinese motifs.
Kyoto	Stylised coloured flower-heads amid blue and gold foliage.
Mikado	Central design featuring two flying herons amid water lily flowers and large leaves. Border of panels containing small birds and stylised plum blossom.
Ming	Chinese junk in a watery landscape.
Oriental Birds	Exotic birds perched on a tree in an Oriental landscape.
Prunus	Prunus flowers on a dark blue ground.
Shan Tung	Central landscape with tree in foreground and three roofed house in background, right. Chinese junk in distance, left. Border as for *Mikado*.
Sheraton	Large pink and orange peony flowers on a dark blue ground.
Arras	Pomegranates, sprays of pink bell-shaped flowers and leaves in shades of green (Plate 12). Designed by Charlotte Rhead. This pattern was later made by Bursley Ltd.
Orion Ware	This was a range of printed wares decorated with naturalistic or stylised flowers and foliage introduced by Frederick Rhead in 1913. Known examples feature naturalistic irises on a buff ground and yellow narcissi grouped in pairs.[17]

Wood & Sons Tube-lined Patterns

Elers	Bands of pairs of stylised leaf forms with projecting pairs of stems from which hang three pendants (Plate 9). Some, presumably early, examples are marked with an F. A.Rhead facsimile signature.
Trellis	Trellis pattern overlaid with stylised roses and pointed leaves (Plate 7).
Check	Chequered pattern in two bands, the upper with small stylised peony flowers (Fig 32).
Mercian Guild	Band of square stylised roses alternating with tubed dots. This rare design may have been made for a special order.
	Bands of triangular leaves and spiralling stems alternating with large tubed dots surrounded by small dots. One example is known marked *Elers*.

These patterns appear to have been based on designs by Charles Rennie Mackintosh. They can all be attributed to Frederick Rhead. The remaining Wood's tube-lined wares, listed below, were the work of Charlotte Rhead.

> Plaque depicting a Japanese female figure playing a shamisen. Known with both a plain blue and a printed Prunus pattern border (Fig 33).
> Plaque, pair to above, depicting a seated Japanese female figure holding a letter in her left hand.

The design appears in various colour arrangements. Plain blue or printed Prunus pattern border (Fig 34). Large yellow tulip-heads with red lobed centres on thick stems with three pointed leaves in two shades of green, surrounded by small five-petalled stylised blue flower heads. This pattern can be attributed to Charlotte Rhead on stylistic grounds, though an example is known with an unusual 'toy drum' backstamp and marked F. A.Rhead.

Persian	Stylised spiky leaves in shades of blue and green embellished with gold on a white ground above a mazarine blue base (Plate 10).
	Band of large red peony flowers and sprays of veined leaves.
Rhodian	Large red flowers with spiky petals and yellow centres on green stems. Leaves in two shades of blue.
Seed Poppy	Open red poppy flowers with blue seeds and green spiky leaves (Plate 11).

Bursley Ltd. printed patterns.

No pattern numbers but backstamps usually incorporate pattern names.

Sylvan	Blue striped four-petalled stylised flowers against a blue ground decorated with stylised lotus flowers in blue and white on an orange ground and bands of overlapping florets in white with orange centres (Plate 16).
Amstel	Birds perched on irregular rock-like forms amid leaves and irregular swirling shapes in shades of brown, blue, dark green and black (Plate 19).
Bagdad	Stylised lotus flowers in blue and white on an orange ground and bands of overlapping florets in white with orange centres (Plate 18).
Benares	Irregular swirling forms in brown and white on a ground of multiple stylised blue flower-heads (Plate 16).
Merton	Lobed leaves in shades of blue and green with blue pointed leaf forms on a reddish brown ground (Plate 16).
Red Parrot	Parrot with outstretched wings in shades of red, orange and green on a blue ground amid circular fruits in orange and mauve (Plate 19). This pattern appears to have been made mainly for the retailer Hales, Hancock and Godwin.
Yellow Parrot	As above, but parrot coloured predominantly in yellow. Introduced in January 1926.
	No name or number. Blue four-petalled stylised flowers with brown or blue centres and stylised leaf and fruit forms in shades of blue and brown on a white ground. Bursley backstamp.

Bursley Ltd – Numbered Patterns.

Pattern Number

25	Tube-lined stylised harebells and yellow flower-heads
28	*Seed Poppy*. Tube-lined open red poppy flowers and blue seeds with green spiky leaves (Plate 11).
29	Tube-lined grapes, asters and circular fruits on stems, blue ground. Closely resembles pattern 456 *Pomona*.
194	Tube-lined naturalistic pansies.
267	Tube-lined stylised dahlias with shaded white petals and stems; powder blue ground.
268	Tube-lined stylised flower-heads in baskets; powder blue ground (Plate 14).
271	*Laredo*. Tube-lined grapes and other fruits and flower heads; blue ground.
324	Tube-lined band of stylised multi-coloured fruits and leaves; various coloured grounds.
326	*Winter Time*. Printed snow scene with robins. Table ware and vases.
411	*Dragon*. Printed dragon pattern designed by Frederick Rhead; finished with various coloured lustred grounds (Plate 21).
426	Tube-lined variation of no. 324.
439	Tube-lined stylised leaf and berry design finished with orange and yellow lustres.
442	Printed and painted pattern. Stylised leaf form perhaps of Middle East inspiration.
443	As no. 442, but tube-lined and lustred.
451	Printed pattern. Stylised flower and leaf design by Frederick Rhead. Lustre ground (Plate 20).
456	*Pomona*. Tube-lined design with pomegranates, grapes and asters on leafy stems (Plate 12). A popular pattern, produced in several enamelled and lustred finishes. Mentioned in the trade press several times between 1922 and 1927.
458	*Pagoda Ware*. Printed pattern with pagoda and other Chinese motifs. Red ground.
459	As no. 458, but blue ground (Plate 21).
471	*Arabian*. Stylised leaves and flowers in powder blue and dark blue. See also nos.648 and 649 (Plate 22).
522	Tube-lined design. Four-petalled stylised flowers and large ribbed leaves. Painted or lustred ground.
577	Tube-lined design. Band of circular fruits in pink, red and yellow on leafy stems (Plate 25).
585	Tube-lined design. Bunches of grapes, brown speckled leaves and brown ribbons on a blue or red ground (Plate 23).
590	"Conventionally treated fruit and leaf design." Perhaps printed.
593	Tube-lined design. Band of multi-coloured fruits on a lustred ground. Various coloured finishes.
606	Printed design (?). Groundwork of brown, relieved with sprays of green and blue.
648	*Arabian*. As for no. 471, but dark blue flowers and leaves outlined in gold (Plate 22).
649	*Arabian*. As for no. 471, but dark blue flowers and leaves with white embellishments on a gold ground.
707	Tube-lined confronted birds and stylised flowers.
726	Tube-lined trellis pattern with circular orange or red fruits and leafy branches in alternate trellis intersections; introduced c1926 (Plate 13).

730	Tube-lined stylised fruits, leaves and stems on a red lustre ground; variation of no. 577.

730   Tube-lined stylised fruits, leaves and stems on a red lustre ground; variation of no. 577.

731   "A leaf pattern worked up in the clay, coloured brown and blue with a rich orange lustre over it". [18] From this description, presumably a tube-lined design.

735   This red lustred pattern (Plate 25) appears to be identical to no. 730. Also known with fruits and leaves outlined in gilt; stems only tube-lined.

736   Variation of no. 577; white ground (Plate 26).

740   Tube-lined "conventional fruit design, restrainedly lustred in a silver-grey". [19] Perhaps another variation of no. 577.

772   Printed design. Stylised multi-coloured fruits. White ground.

817   Printed design. "A yellow ground with tangerine and purple grapes decoration." [20]

878   Printed design. Fish swimming amid vegetation. Blue and white ground.

907   *Mikado*. Printed design, painted onglaze with peonies, stylised flowers and Chinese motifs.

917   Blue stylised leaves outlined in gold on a white ground. Similar to *Arabian* (no. 648).

982   Printed design. Stylised veined circular seed heads (pomegranates?).

986   Printed design. Stylised flower heads and fruits on a blue ground.

1087   *Selah Ware*. Birds on fruiting and leafy branches, painted onglaze. Blue ground.

1189   Tube-lined chrysanthemums, flower heads and multi-coloured butterflies on a dark blue ground (sandwich sets only?).

1274   *Pomme d'Or*. Also known as *Golden Apple*. Printed design of multi-coloured circular fruits and green leaves in sprays within a crazed border. Ivory or red central ground. Table wares. Pattern no. 1289 appears to be a tubed version of this design (see below).

1288   Tube-lined band of stylised leaves and speckled fruits on a mazarine ground.

1289   Tube-lined circular multi-coloured fruits between geometric shapes; blue and white ground. See also no. 1274.

1325   Tube-lined design of speckled circular fruits similar to no. 1288 but with onglaze overpainted black panels of Oriental inspiration by Horace Wain (see next).

1326   As no. 1325, but with red overpainted panels.

1327   Variation of no. 1325. An example is known with the panel painting omitted.

1419   Tube-lined stylised brown and cream peonies and other flowers, with blue leaves and berries enclosing shaped chinoiserie panels. The panels perhaps by Horace Wain.

1420   Tube-lined peonies in orange and fawn amid variously shaped blue leaves with gold ribs. See also nos.1432 and 1548.

1432   As for no. 1420. Brown peonies tubed in blue, with dark blue and buff leaves (Plate 27).

1495   Tube-lined black grapes and vine leaves.

1501(?) Printed and painted table ware. Yellow and blue water lilies and green leaves on a black ground.

1543   Stylised flower heads in pink and red with elongated brown and green leaves. Blue ground.

1548   As for nos.1420 and 1432, but orange and red flowers. Pale blue ground.

1550   Open poppy flowers in red, orange, blue and buff with long spiky deep blue leaves on a green or yellow ground (Plate 28).

1553(?) Tube-lined stylised flower-heads, grapes and spiky leaves.

1554   Tube-lined clusters of small berries with gold and blue ribbed leaves. Blue ground.

1556   Tube-lined stylised birds in red, blue and gold, flower-heads and geometric devices.

1574   Tube-lined multi-coloured poppy seed-heads on stiff stems with spiky blue leaves (Plate 24).

1627   Tube-lined stylised orange, yellow, blue and mauve flower-heads with blue and green ribbed leaves. White ground.

1713   Tube-lined plaque, the central device a two-bodied animal with a single head (a fox?), similar to no. 1737, within a border of stylised leaves and oval flower heads.

1714   Tube-lined plaque; central female figure in profile surrounded by panels enclosing stylised foliage.

1732   *Geisha*. Printed tableware design; red-breasted bird perched on flowering grassy stems. Designed by Jack Butler.

1736A Plaque with central device of a fantastic bird with long neck and open wings painted in copper lustre, within 21 ovoid panels enclosing painted and tube-lined elongated leaves. This piece, probably a trial, and no. 1737, were attributed to Frederick Rhead by the late Bert Heath of Sydney, Australia. Mr. Heath worked for Bursley Ltd. in the early 1920s.

1737   Tube-lined plaque with central device of a two-bodied animal with a single head (similar to 1713) within a border of grotesques and roundels containing stylised foliage. Attributed to Frederick Rhead (see 1736A).

1739   Tube-lined plaque with central device of a grotesque within a border of panels of alternate interlinking heart-shapes and stylised lotus plants.

1740   Tube-lined plaque with central device of a lion rampant outlined in copper within a border of stylised flower forms.

1746   Painted plaque with the arms of the former Middlesbrough County Borough. The arms were granted on 8 November 1911.

1775A Tube-lined stylised flower-heads in pink, yellow and gold on trailing stems with elongated ribbed leaves.

1793   Tube-lined open multi-coloured flower-heads with spiky leaves.

1859   Painted plaque depicting the galleon *Santa Maria* on a choppy blue sea.

1876   Galleon in a seascape before a setting sun on a blue and white striped sea, tubed in blue, black and brown. Some versions have a Wood & Sons backstamp. Perhaps designed by Jack Butler (Plate 96).

1917	Tube-lined bunches of red and pink berries and stylised flower-heads.

1917   Tube-lined bunches of red and pink berries and stylised flower-heads.
1952   Tube-lined plaque with central stylised flower surrounded by carnations and tulips. Dark blue border with stylised flower-heads and gold plant forms. Attributed by family tradition to Charlotte Rhead.
1973   Printed blue flower-heads.
1974   *Vert de Mer Series.* Tube-lined stylised flower-heads and geometric forms. Perhaps designed by Jack Butler (Plate 29).
1975   Tube-lined flower baskets in blue and orange each containing six flower-heads.
1987   Blue tubed stylised flowers with bunches of small flower-heads on stems. Various coloured flowers and grounds.
2059   Stylised floral design with green and blue leaves on a pink ground decorated with spirals.
2102   Tube-lined castle in a watery landscape viewed under a leafy branch with festoons of stylised orange flowers. Designer unidentified.
2542   *Floretta.* Naturalistic sprays of apple blossom painted on-glaze (Plate 29).

Backstamps

Backstamp 1 – Wood & Sons, mark used on Pâte-sur-Pâte wares 1913 onwards.

Backstamp 2 – Wood & Sons, mark used on Elers pattern ware (tube-lined) 1913 onwards.

Backstamp 3 – Wood & Sons, mark used on Trellis pattern ware (tube-lined) 1913 onwards.

Backstamp 4 – Wood & Sons, Yuan; typical mark used on printed wares 1915 onwards.

Backstamp 5 – Bursley Ltd, c1925.

Backstamp 6 – Wood & Sons, Seed Poppy mark, c1921.

Backstamp 7 – Bursley Ltd, c1921.

Backstamp 8 – Wood & Sons, typical Cosy Pot mark, c1922.

Backstamp 6 – Bursley Ltd, c1927(?).

Backstamp 7 – Bursley Ltd, c1929.

Backstamp 8 – Hales, Hancock & Godwin, mark used on items made specially for this retailer.

Backstamp 9 – Amstel, typical mark used on Frederick Rhead's printed designs for Bursley Ltd., c1923.

Backstamp 10 – Ellgreave Pottery Co. Ltd., Lottie Rhead Ware, c1923.

Plate 2 Wileman & Co. Faience plaque with tube-lined and sgraffito decoration. Pattern 11052A, designed by Frederick Rhead. Value £325/$635.

Plate 3 Wardle & Co. Jardinière, probably designed by Frederick Hurten Rhead and tube-lined by Charlotte or Dollie Rhead. Value £450/$880.

Plate 4 Tiles designed by Frederick Rhead and tube-lined by Charlotte or Dollie Rhead. Tile in frame £400/$780; others £300/$585 each.

Plate 1: Wileman & Co. Urbato vase with tube-lined decoration. Pattern no.4056, designed by Frederick Rhead. Value £450/$880.

Plate 5 Wardle & Co. Candlestick, probably designed by Frederick Hurten Rhead and tube-lined by Charlotte or Dollie Rhead. £200/$390.

Plate 6 Wardle & Co. Vases designed by Harry Rhead. £300/$585 each.

Plate 7 Wood & Sons. Trellis pattern, candlestick £450/$880, double gourd vase £300/$585 and 'Cosy' pot £200/$390.

Plate 8 Wood & Sons. Pâte-sur-pâte vases designed by Frederick Rhead. £500/$975 each.

Plate 9 Wood & Sons. Elers pattern, tray for trinket set and ginger jar, £350/$685.

Plate 10 Wood & Sons. Vase, Persian pattern. £325/$635.

Plate 11 Wood & Sons. Bottle £375/$730 and 'Cosy' pot, Seed Poppy pattern £250/$490.

Plate 12 Bursley Ltd. Vases tubed with the Pomona pattern (no. 456), c1922, and Wood & Sons vase with the Arras printed pattern (in centre), c1917. Charlotte Rhead reused many of the Arras motifs later on Pomona. £200-£300/$390-$585 each.

Plate 13 Wood & Sons. Yuan 'Cosy' pot. Bursley Ltd. 'Cosy' pot, pattern no. 726. £200-£300/$390-$585 each.

Plate 14 Bursley Ltd., pattern no. 268. £450/$880.

Plate 15 Wood & Sons. Kang-Hi pattern, ginger jar. £1200/$2340.

Plate 16 Bursley Ltd. Merton £300/$585, Benares £150/$295 and Sylvan patterns £200/$390.

Plate 17 Ellgreave Pottery Co. Ltd., cup, saucer and jug, Lottie Rhead Ware. £75/$145 each.

Plate 18 Bursley Ltd. Bagdad pattern. £350/$685 each.

Plate 19 Bursley Ltd. The popular Amstel pattern and Red Parrot, made for the retailer Hales, Hancock and Godwin. £180-£250/$350-$490 each.

Plate 20 Bursley Ltd., pattern no. 451. £300/$585.

Plate 21 Bursley Ltd., Dragon (no. 411) vase £175/$340, coffee pot £125/$245 and, at back, Pagoda (no. 459) £150/$295.

Plate 22 Bursley Ltd., Arabian (no. 471).Vase £325/$635, plate £375/$730.

Plate 23 Bursley Ltd., pattern no. 585. From left £250/$490, and £320/$625.

Plate 24 Bursley Ltd., pattern no. 1574. £300/$585.

Plate 25 Bursley Ltd., pattern nos. 577, £150/$295, and 735, £260/$505.

Plate 26 Bursley Ltd., pattern no. 736. £350/$685.

Plate 27 Bursley Ltd., pattern no. 1432. £300/$585 each.

Plate 28 Bursley Ltd., pattern no. 1550. From left £250/$490 and £350/$685.

Plate 29 Bursley Ltd., pattern 1974 (Vert de Mer series) £175/$340 and pattern 2542, Floretta £300/$585.

Plate 30 Burgess & Leigh pattern 4100, Sylvan. £550/$1075.

Plate 31 Burgess & Leigh pattern 4016. From left £400/$780, £500/$975 and £300/$585.

Plate 32 Burgess & Leigh patterns 4071 £200/$390 and 4113 £250/$490.

PLATE 6.

BURGESS & LEIGH, LTD., Middleport Pottery, BURSLEM.

Deco. 3973.

Deco. 3973.

Deco. 4001.

Deco. 4001.

"Rose Bowl"

Vase 48

Vase 42.

Deco. 4001.

"Chinese Bowl"

Vase 50.

Vase 68.

Deco. 4016.

Deco. 4016.

"Warwick" Flower Pot.

Vase 35.

Vase 76.

"Regent" Floating Bowl.

Vase 69.

Deco. 3961.

Deco. 3934.

"Kew" Floating Bowl. 3990.

Vase 77.

Vase 74.

Vase 73.

Vase 52.

"Beverley" Fruit Bowl Deco. 3934.

Sq. Spill. 3961.

"Avon" Fruit Bowl Deco. 4002.

"Burleigh" Art Ware.

Plate 33 Page from a Burgess & Leigh catalogue, c.1927 showing several of Charlotte Rhead's early designs for the company.

Plate 34 Burgess & Leigh pattern 4001, Gouda. £450/$880.

Plate 35 Burgess & Leigh pattern 4100, Sylvan. £500/$975.

Plate 36 Burgess & Leigh patterns 4102 and 4105. £350/$685 set.

Plate 37 Burgess & Leigh patterns 4101, £300/$585, Garland and 4789, £250/$490 Laurel Band.

Plate 38 Burgess & Leigh pattern 4118. £2000/$3900.   *Plate 39 Burgess & Leigh pattern 4012. £2000/$3900.*

Plate 40 Burgess & Leigh pattern 4120, Carnival. From left £375/$730, £650/$1270.

Plate 41 Burgess & Leigh pattern 3973.

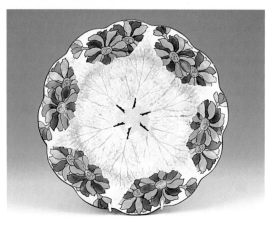

Plate 42 Burgess & Leigh pattern 4116. £250/$490.

Plate 43 Burgess & Leigh pattern 4347, New Vine. £250/$490.

Plate 44 Burgess & Leigh pattern 4111. £2200/$4290.

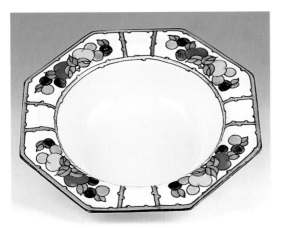

Plate 45 Burgess & Leigh pattern 4367, a colour variation of Rutland. £100/$195.

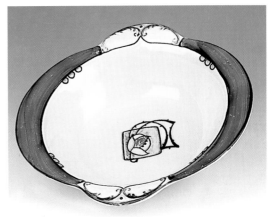

Plate 46 Burgess & Leigh pattern 4471, an example of a tubed pattern on an item of suite ware. £85/$165.

Plate 47 Burgess & Leigh pattern 4752, Florentine. From left, £325/$635, £450/$880 and £250/$490.

Plate 48 Crown Ducal pattern 2681, Byzantine.

Plate 49 Crown Ducal patterns Granada 3321, £350/$685; 2682 £200/$390; and Primula, £175/$340.

Plate 50 Crown Ducal patterns 3274, Stitch (left) with 4088 and 4903, variations of Patch. It is not always possible to identify the pattern numbers of these simple designs as many colour variations were employed over the years. £80-£150/$155-$295 each.

Plate 51 Crown Ducal pattern 2691, Turin. From left £275/$535, £300/$585, £200/$390, and £150/$295.

Plate 52 Crown Ducal pattern 3637, Padua. £250/$490.

Plate 53 Crown Ducal children's ware, patterns 3131 (Chicks), 3133 (Little Boy Blue) and Polly (no pattern number). £275/$535 each

Plate 54 Crown Ducal pattern 3052, Persino. £275/$535.

Plate 55 Crown Ducal pattern 3797, Hydrangea. £320/$625.

Plate 56 Crown Ducal pattern 3272, Rhodian. £275/$525.

Plate 57 Crown Ducal pattern 2800. £250/$490.

Plate 58 Crown Ducal pattern 4016, Blue Peony. £350/$685.

Plate 59 Crown Ducal pattern 4036, Omar. £900/$1755.

Plate 60 Prototype of pattern 4511, Manchu, tubed by Charlotte Rhead. £1500/$2925.

Plate 61 Crown Ducal pattern 4100. £350/$685.

Plate 62 Crown Ducal patterns 3727, £130/$255, 5728, £80/$155 and 6568, £120/$235.

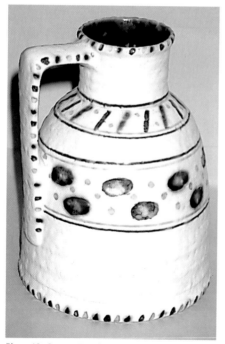

Plate 63 Crown Ducal pattern 4518. This design, probably by Charlotte Rhead, was not tube-lined but 'carved in the clay'. £150/$295.

Plate 64 Crown Ducal pattern 4040, £350/$685, Persian Rose (at back), £550/$1075 and 4300, Tudor Rose, £275/$535.

Plate 65 Crown Ducal pattern 4040, Persian Rose £350/$685, bottom left, and, clockwise, Tudor Rose variations patterns 4318, £450/$880, 5393, £250/$490, and 4491, £220/$430. The pattern number for the small jug in front £180/$350, is uncertain.

Plate 66 Crown Ducal patterns 2682 and 4795.

Plate 67 Crown Ducal pattern 4921, GoldenLeaves. From left £135/$265, £95/$185, £170/$330.

Plate 68 Crown Ducal pattern 4511, Green Dragon, better known as Manchu. From left £250/$490, £350/$685, £225/$440, £350/$685, and at back £375/$730.

Plate 69 Crown Ducal patterns 4521, £175/$340 and 4794, £275/$535.

Plate 70 Crown Ducal patterns 4724 (red/white), £300/$585 and 4525 (blue/white) £250/$490. Commemorative wares for the coronation of Edward VIII and, after his abdication, George VI.

Plate 71 Crown Ducal pattern 4922, Florian. £450/$880.

Plate 72 Crown Ducal pattern 4921, GoldenLeaves. £200/$390.

Plate 73 Crown Ducal pattern 4924, Carnation. £350/$685.

Plate 74 Crown Ducal pattern 4925, Arabian Scroll. £400/$780.

Plate 75 Crown Ducal pattern 5391, Persian Leaf. £275/$535.

Plate 76 Crown Ducal pattern 4953, Foxglove. £475/$925.

Plate 77 Crown Ducal pattern 4954, Wisteria. £475/$925.

Plate 78 Crown Ducal pattern 5983, Ankara. £350/$685.

Plate 79 Crown Ducal pattern 5627, Tarragona. £275/$535.

Plate 80 Crown Ducal pattern 5803, Palermo. £275/$535.

Plate 81 Crown Ducal pattern 5411, Caliph. £550/$1075.

Plate 82 Crown Ducal pattern 5802, Fruit Border. £300/$585.

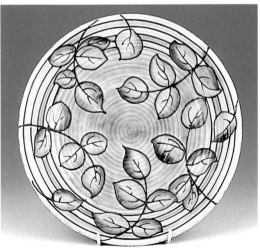

Plate 83 Royal Cauldon Autumn Leaves pattern. Designed by Edith Gaiter, this tubed design was evidently intended to compete with the very successful Crown Ducal Golden Leaves pattern (see plates 67 and 72). £100/$195.

Plate 84 Crown Ducal patterns 7377, £60/$115, Leaf and Trellis (not Charlotte Rhead) and 5982, £100/$195, Circular Fruits.

Plate 85 Crown Ducal patterns 6564, £80/$155 and 5983, £80/$155 Ankara, probably a post-war version.

Plate 86 Crown Ducal plaque, pattern 4016, Blue Peony.
£375/$730.

Plate 87 Crown Ducal patterns 6016 Trellis, £220/$430, 2800,
£275/$535 and 6189 Mexican, £150/$295.

Plate 88 Crown Ducal pattern 6778. £125/$245.

Plate 89 Crown Ducal patterns 6884, Pink Oyster, £50/$100 and
6904, £80/$155. Both post war. Not Charlotte Rhead.

Bursley Ware

640/5
T.L. 43

CIGARETTE BOX 693
T.L. 40

SWEET 692
T.L. 40

PLAQUE
T.L. 5

BOWL 682. M/s
T.L. 2

BASKET No I
T.L. 3

BASKET 405/2
T.L. 14

JUG 462
T.L. 4

JUG 673. M/s
T.L. 76

VASE 672
T.L. 38

Plate 90 H. J. Wood, Ltd. catalogue, c.1954.

Plate 91 H. J. Wood, Ltd. Bursley Ware patterns T.L. 2, T.L. 12 , T.L. 4 (ashtray) and T.L. 37. From left £300/$585, £70/$135, £120/$235 and lamp base at back £300/$585.

Plate 92 H. J. Wood, Ltd. Bursley Ware patterns T.L. 4, T.L. 5 and T.L. 40. £250/$490 each.

Plate 93 H. J. Wood, Ltd. Bursley Ware patterns T.L. 14, £275/$535 and T.L. 76, £200/$390.

Plate 94 Top: Crown Ducal pattern 4511, £250/$490, Manchu. Middle: Crown Ducal plaque, pattern 6189, £300/$585. Crown Ducal plaque pattern 6904, £200/$390, post war, not by Charlotte Rhead. Crown Ducal plaque pattern 4040, £350/$685. Bottom: Crown Ducal plaque perhaps a version of pattern 2681 Byzantine, £275/$535. Crown Ducal plaque, pattern 5411 Caliph, £550/$1075.

Plate 95 Top: Crown Ducal plaque, pattern 5983, £350/$685, Ankara. H. J. Wood ginger jar, pattern T.L. 3. £325/$635, Crown Ducal vase, pattern 6016, £250/$490, Trellis. Middle: Crown Ducal vase, pattern 3272, Rhodian (colour variation); Crown Ducal vase, pattern 4795. £150/$295, Crown Ducal flower jug, pattern 2681, Byzantine, £250/$490. Bottom: Crown Ducal vase, pattern 4795, £150/$295. Burgess & Leigh vase, pattern 4100, Sylvan, £175/$340, H. J. Wood toast rack, pattern T. L. 3, £125/$245.

Plate 96 Top: Crown Ducal plaque, pattern 4298. H. J. Wood vase, pattern T. L. 3. Middle: Crown Ducal plaque, pattern 3272, Rhodian. Wood & Sons plaque, pattern 1876, not designed by Charlotte Rhead. Bottom: Crown Ducal flower jug, pattern 4016, Blue Peony. Crown Ducal vase, pattern 4921 Golden Leaves, jug with unknown pattern.

Plate 97 Top: Crown Ducal vase, pattern 3272 Rhodian. Crown Ducal vase, pattern 4040 Persian Rose. Crown Ducal flower jug, pattern 6189 Mexican. Middle: Crown Ducal flower jug, pattern 4016 Blue Peony. H. J. Wood flower jug, pattern T.L. 37 Daisy. Crown Ducal vase, pattern 4300 Tudor Rose. Corwn Ducal vase, pattern 3321 Granada. Crown Ducal vase, pattern 6189 Mexican. Bottom: Crown Ducal vase, pattern 2681 Byzantine. H. J. Wood vase, pattern T.L. 2, Crown Ducal flower vase, pattern 4016 Blue Peony. Crown Ducal vase, pattern 6189 Mexican. Pair Crown Ducal vases, pattern 2691 Turin. £125-£450/$245-$880 each.

Plate 98 H. J. Wood Ltd, Bursley Ware plaque pattern T.L. 95, designed by Eddie Sambrook. £375/$730.

Plate 99 H. J. Wood Ltd, Bursley Ware plaque pattern T.L. 118, designed by Jessie Tait. £200/$390.

Plate 100 H. J. Wood Ltd, Bursley Ware plaque pattern T.L. 31. £450/$880.

Plate 101 Crown Ducal plaque, pattern 6189, Mexican. £375/$730.

Plate 102 Crown Ducal plaque, pattern 4040, Perisan Rose, unusual variation. £550/$1075.

Plate 103 Crown Ducal plaque, pattern 3272, Rhodian, variation with coloured leaves. £450/$880.

Plate 104 H. J. Wood Ltd, Bursley Ware plaque pattern T.L. 43. £375/$730.

Plate 105 H. J. Wood Ltd, Bursley Ware plaque pattern T.L. 76. £275/$535.

Plate 106 Burgess & Leigh pattern 4752, Florentine. £450/$880.

Plate 107 Crown Ducal plaque, pattern 3321, Granada. £500/$975.

Plate 108 Crown Ducal plaque, pattern 7377, Leaf & Trellis, a post-war production not by Charlotte Rhead. £175/$340.

Plate 109 Crown Ducal plaque, pattern 5803, Palermo. £375/$730.

Plate 110 Crown Ducal flower jug, pattern 5803, Palermo. £280/$545.

Plate 111 H. J. Wood Ltd, Bursley Ware plaque pattern T.L. 14. £375/$730.

Plate 112 H. J. Wood Ltd, Bursley Ware plaque pattern T.L. 14. Note edge bands. £450/$880.

Plate 113 H. J. Wood Ltd, Bursley Ware plaque pattern T.L. 37, Daisy. £450/$880.

Plate 114 Wileman faience plaque, pattern 11049B. £275/$535.

Plate 115 Crown Ducal children's plate, pattern 3132, Is it carrots?. £275/$535.

Plate 116 H. J. Wood Ltd, Bursley Ware bowl pattern T.L. 40. £250/$490.

Plate 117 Crown Ducal vase and flower jug pattern 2691, Turin. £200/$390 each.

Plate 118 H. J. Wood Ltd, Bursley Ware vase pattern T.L. 38, £450/$880. The pattern on the ginger jar on the right, T.L. 39, £175/$340, is not by Charlotte Rhead.

Plate 119 Wood & Sons tube-lined vase, Elers pattern. £350/$685.

Plate 120 H. J. Wood Ltd, Bursley Ware wall plaques pattern T.L. 40C. £250-£300/$490-$585 pair.

Plate 121 Wood & Sons pâte-sur-päte vase. £750/$1465.

80

Burgess & Leigh

By the end of 1926 Charlotte Rhead had left Wood's and its associated companies, Bursley Ltd. and the Ellgreave Pottery Co., and joined the nearby firm of Burgess & Leigh, makers of Burleigh Ware, at the Middleport Pottery in Burslem. There is a superficial resemblance between the names Bursley and Burleigh which can be confusing. Moreover Charlotte's early designs for Burgess & Leigh often made use of the same motifs she had used at Wood's – black grapes, for example, pomegranates, poppies and anemones. But the shapes to which these decorations were applied are different, and the backstamps used by the two firms, quite distinctive.

Fig 37 Aerial view of Burgess & Leigh's Middleport Pottery in Burslem. The photograph was taken shortly before Charlotte Rhead joined the company in 1926.

Burgess & Leigh was a private firm owned and managed by members of the Leigh family. The Middleport Pottery, built in 1889 and backing on to the Trent and Mersey canal, had been carefully designed so that the various processes would flow smoothly into each other. An aerial view, taken in the 1920s, shows the building as it must have appeared about the time Charlotte started work there (Fig 37). It looks much the same today, though only one bottle kiln now remains.

The Leighs must have known the Rhead family for a long time and it was a member of the Leigh family, Edmund Leigh, who presented the Gladstone Vase to the Liberal leader and sometime prime minister, William Ewart Gladstone, on behalf of the Burslem Liberals at Hawarden Castle in 1888. This vase was designed and decorated in *pâte-sur-pâte* by Charlotte's father, Frederick, and was his *chef d'oeuvre*. Charlotte's new job had probably been arranged by Charles Wilkes, the head modeller at Burgess & Leigh. Wilkes, who seems to have been fond of Charlotte, was a close family friend of the Rheads and used to play bridge with them regularly. He and Frederick cooperated in setting up a small pottery in Burslem to produce ornamental items, a venture which apparently did not meet with much success.

Charlotte was evidently considered to be an important acquisition by Burgess & Leigh as the company took a full-page advertisement in the March 1927 issue of *The Pottery Gazette* to announce her arrival, describing her as "the accomplished lady artist", adding "who has produced for us a number of original decorations, all pure HANDCRAFT Combining grace and dignity of design with the most beautiful *under the glaze* colourings".[1] A special display, it was noted, was on view in the firm's London showroom.

Burgess & Leigh had not made tube-lined productions before Charlotte's arrival so she would have had to start by recruiting and training staff in this new skill. She evidently made a good job of it for by March 1927 around fourteen different designs were being produced. Most of these early lines were described in some detail in the pattern book although they are not illustrated or dated. Even the later entries, by several different hands and often extremely brief, make it possible to chart Charlotte's work for this company fairly comprehensively. The trade press also gave Burgess & Leigh good publicity, illustrating a number of Charlotte's designs and these reference help to date her patterns. Every pattern which was entered in the pattern book was allocated a four-figure number and this number can usually – though unfortunately not invariably – be found on the base of each object.

The earliest of Charlotte's patterns seems to have been no. 3973. It consists of a band of tube-lined anemones, in various colours, on a plain blue ground. The vases decorated with this pattern also have a broad black band above the anemones (Plate 34). As might be expected, this and several other early patterns show a distinct family resemblance to Charlotte Rhead's Bursley Ware designs. The anemones on pattern no. 3973, for instance, appeared on several previous occasions, most notably on the Bursley *Pomona* pattern (Plate 12). A catalogue issued by Burgess & Leigh in about 1927 illustrates some of these earlier patterns (Plate 33).

Among the early designs not featured in the catalogue were several elaborate wall plaques with rich decorations, such as the pheasant and pomegranate pattern illustrated in Plate 39, while another, more exotic, design featured a seated Japanese girl holding a letter. Charlotte had earlier used the same Japanese design, though with the image reversed, for a tube-lined plaque at Wood's (Fig 34); its source was probably an unidentified Japanese print. Although these Burgess & Leigh productions were intended for sale, they must have been very expensive, the cost of tubing alone for the pheasant and pomegranate design being assessed at twenty-four shillings, a large sum at the time. No doubt Charlotte herself would have executed this complicated work and it seem likely that only very small numbers, perhaps no more than half a dozen of each design, were produced.

Burgess & Leigh provided Charlotte with a large room in the Middleport Pottery where she could work and simultaneously supervise the tube-liners. She always wore a clean smock of her own design and making, and was usually accompanied by her little dog, to whom he a devoted. She would give this dog saucers of milk, a cause of some misunderstanding as some of the company employees thought she was providing the milk for the benefit of the resident mice! While she was at Burgess & Leigh Charlotte took a long holiday, probably to visit her brothers in America. She was able to do this as her sister Dollie almost literally stepped into her shoes, taking time off from her midwifery to deputise for her at the Middleport Pottery. Dollie is said to have acted in this capacity most competently, showing that she had not forgotten her skills as a tube-liner.

As time went on Charlotte's patterns tended to become simpler, though they continued to feature her favourite motifs, fruit and flowers. Fruits in particular, with their rounded forms, were a satisfying decoration and easy to tube-line. Consequently wares thus ornamented were economical to make. Charlotte was a practical potter who appreciated as much as anyone the need to keep down production costs and yet to design attractive pieces. So we find *The Pottery Gazette* drawing shopkeepers attention to the virtues of her Garland pattern (Plate 37) as "lines one might safely put before a customer who desires to make a respectable gift without embarking on more than a modest outlay".[2]

Charlotte always paid careful attention to the way her designs fitted the various shapes as well as to the way they were coloured. At first much of the decoration was applied underglaze – a speciality which the company had emphasised in its advertisement announcing Charlotte's arrival. Later however she seems to have increasingly favoured the use of onglaze enamels and broken or mottled glazes. She also favoured the use of lustres as her father had done when she worked with him at the Crown Pottery. Lustres, though, do not wear well and care is needed in purchasing many of the pieces she designed for Burgess & Leigh. Take, for example, one of the first patterns she produced for the company using lustres, no. 4016 (Plate 31). This is an attractive design with lustred bands, top and bottom, over a tubed fruit pattern, and it must have been popular, to judge by the number of pieces which can still be found. But not all these pieces are in good condition now as the lustres have often deteriorated, the interiors of bowls in particular having worn. It was perhaps for this reason that Charlotte turned her attention to the more durable onglaze enamels.

Most of Charlotte's designs for the firm were tube-lined but she also supplied some attractive painted and printed examples. One pattern, for instance, no. 4567, which has a crossed sticks and daisy motif, was produced both as a print, for tea and dinner ware, and in a tube-lined form for the ornamental pieces. In the 1920s her palette was often brightly coloured, in accordance with the taste of the time. The yellow and coral used on the *Carnival* pattern is a case in point. This is a particularly interesting design as it resembles a giant flower when seen on the inside of a bowl and yet appears more like a sunburst when viewed on the side of a vase; both these effects can be seen in Plate 40. The vibrant colours of *Carnival* may have been intended to compete with Clarice Cliff's *Bizarre* designs which were gaining popularity at the time, as were the bright patterns introduced by Susie Cooper at Gray's.

By the early 1930s the changes in Charlotte's style had become more pronounced. She was now producing simpler designs in which sombre colours and subdued lustres combined with broken or mottled glazes predominate. A good example of this trend is provided by her *Florentine* design (Plate 47) which must have been made in considerable quantity and used on a great many shapes – to judge by the large number of pieces which still exist. Indeed, *Florentine* is the Burgess & Leigh pattern which collectors are now most likely to come across. To some extent these developments may have been due to the depressed economic climate at the time in the aftermath of the Wall Street Crash of 1929. But there may have been other more personal factors, too. In that same summer, Burgess & Leigh had appointed a new designer, the artist Harold Bennett, to work alongside the aging art director, a man named Leigh. 'Designer Leigh', as he was known – he was no relation to the Leighs who owned the firm – had barely kept pace with the rapid stylistic changes of the 1920s and in any case was due to retire soon. Bennett at once showed himself

Fig 39 Burgess & Leigh pattern no. 4356, Rutland. £450/$880 set.

to be the man Burgess & Leigh needed for their bread-and-butter lines, the dinner, tea and toilet ware. He was very sensitive about his own position, however, and recognising Charlotte's ability, must have considered her a rival and perhaps a threat. He may even have thought of her as a candidate for the post of art director when 'Designer Leigh' had gone, a post he clearly coveted. In the end Charlotte evidently felt that she had to leave, though she took the decision to do so with great reluctance. This was sometime in 1931 and, while the exact circumstances are not known, contemporaries remember her marked distress at the time she left Burgess & Leigh.

Harold Bennett did eventually become art director and in this capacity designed some tube-lined wares for Burgess & Leigh himself during the 1930s. These are sometimes mistaken for Charlotte's work, but for these specialised wares at least he lacked her flair, and his tube-lined patterns are decidedly ordinary when compared to hers. Any tube-lined piece with a pattern number over 5000 can be attributed to him. In addition Bennett's name occasionally appears on the base of examples of Charlotte's popular *Florentine* design which suggests that her patterns at least remained in production for some time after her departure.

Notes for Collectors

When Charlotte Rhead joined Burgess & Leigh, the firm decided to advertise her work by base marking the articles she had designed with her tube-lined 'signature'. This practice, which was current in the Potteries in the 1920s, may have been introduced in order to compete with designers working for other companies, among them Clarice Cliff, Susie Cooper and Molly Hancock, whose names were printed on the bases of their work. Although some of her designs for the Ellgreave Pottery had been marked *Lottie Rhead Ware*, rather surprisingly neither her father's name nor hers had appeared on any of the Bursley Ltd. productions made at the Crown Works, with the exception of the *pâte-sur-pâte*. At Burgess & Leigh the style 'L. Rhead' was adopted, 'L' standing for Lottie, the familiar first name used by her family and friends. On some pieces, particularly the earlier productions and the more elaborate plaques, Charlotte is likely to have tubed the 'signature' herself but this would hardly have been possible for the later mass-produced lines. So it was the tube-liners responsible for the decoration of the pieces who would have added the 'L. Rhead' which can usually be found on the base of her Burgess & Leigh productions. Each tube-liner had her own mark which she would also add. The names and marks of known tube-liners follow these notes, but the list is by no means complete, and it has not even been possible to correlate all the known names and the marks.

Burgess & Leigh were fortunate to have in their employ two talented modellers, Charles Wilkes and Ernest Bailey, and between them they were responsible for most of the shapes that Charlotte was required to decorate. These shapes included about twenty different vases, round and octagonal bowls, some embossed with moulded vine leaves, flowerpots, jardinières, bulb bowls, wall plaques of different sizes and a large range of tableware. The vases were given shape numbers, usually of two digits, which were impressed on their bases, while the bowls were distinguished by names such as Palissy (with a wide undulating rim) and Avon (with a wide octagonal rim, as can be seen in the bottom right corner of Plate 33). Most of these shapes were moulded, but at the time Burgess & Leigh still employed a thrower who worked with a hand-turned wheel. Among the pieces which were hand-thrown was a squat ovoid vase, impressed with the number 76, and some of Charlotte's designs can be found on this shape.

In the late 1920s there was a vogue for sandwich sets which usually consisted of a dish and four or six plates. Burgess & Leigh patented and marketed several different models, among them the Crescent dish which could accommodate six or more stacked triangular plates (Plate 36) and an oblong model with a handle and two compartments named the Richmond. Tube-lined designs were ideal for decorating these sandwich sets and Charlotte made many patterns expressly for this purpose.

Charlotte also provided some designs for utilitarian items which formed the company's stock-in-trade. These included tea and dinner sets and a diverse selection of associated items collectively termed 'suite' ware, the designs for which are noted in the list of patterns that follows. The Sunshine pattern (no. 4609) for example was applied not only to complete dinner services, but to cups, saucers, four sizes of teapot, three different cheese dishes, egg sets, beakers, mugs, teapot stands, trays, oatmeal bowls, scollops, large and small honey pots, cruets, covered butter dishes and toast racks. Other designs were applied to coffee pots, coffee cans and saucers, jugs in several sizes and shapes, biscuit jars and fruit and salad sets. As production must have been considerable, it is perhaps surprising that relatively few of these utilitarian wares have come to light. Indeed, with the exception of a small number of patterns, Charlotte's Burgess & Leigh designs do not come on the market very often.

The list that follows has been taken from the company pattern book which usually specified the shapes to which each pattern was applied, though the book is not illustrated, nor is it comprehensive or always easy to follow. The entries, inevitably, were made by several different hands and some are more specific than others. No indication is given in the pattern book as to whether or not a particular pattern went into commercial production and it is unlikely that all did so.

It was a regular practice for a few samples of a new pattern to be made and given to the firm's travellers to try out on the market and, as a result of their reports, a decision was made as to which designs would go into production. While some of these samples were apparently allocated pattern numbers, others were not. Unmarked pieces which sometimes turn up with patterns that do not appear to fit with any of the pattern book descriptions can be assumed to be samples which did not go into production. It should also be noted that a few pieces have been seen with incorrect pattern numbers – unsurprising, perhaps, in a busy pottery.

There may be one and perhaps two additions to the base marks already noted – the pattern number, shape number where applicable, signature, facsimile or otherwise, and tube-liners mark. These are the Burgess & Leigh backstamp and a painted decorator's mark. Several backstamps were used while Charlotte worked for the company and these are illustrated at the end of the chapter. Particularly confusing is the mark inscribed Lawleys' Norfolk Pottery STOKE which was used on some of her work, mainly sandwich sets, in the late 1920s. In reality such pieces were made at the Middleport Pottery, like all other Burgess & Leigh productions, and were produced specially for Lawleys' retail shops.

Burgess & Leigh Decorators (1926-1931)
Tube-liners and their marks
3   Mary Jackson or Hilda Machin
Ṡ   Perhaps Stella Kerry who was also a lustrer
L.   Lily Marshall?
I.
P
B.   Perhaps a variation of Mary Jackson's mark

Burgess & Leigh Patterns
3973   Band of anemones in shades of blue and red, tubed in black. Perhaps the first pattern designed by Charlotte Rhead for Burgess & Leigh. Vases and useful items (Plate 41). Also illustrated in Burgess & Leigh catalogue of c1927 (Plate 33).

3997   Multicoloured stylised open flower-heads (described in the pattern book as 'Japanese'), orange and yellow leaves and lobed stems, tubed in black. Bowls, yellow inside and out.

3998   Speckled fruits in orange, fawn and pink on red-brown stems. Bowls.

3999   Apples in red, pink and orange, black grapes, green leaves

Fig 38 Burgess & Leigh jardinière, Florentine pattern, no. 4108. This large piece was displayed at the company's London showrooms until World War Two. £1500+/$2925.

and red-brown stems. Sandwich and fruit sets.

4000   Pomegranates, apples and black grapes in shades of pink, yellow and orange, green leaves, brown stems. Fruit sets.

4001   *Gouda* Repeating cloud scroll devices and stylised roses within lobed and pointed panels, painted in purple, pink and orange. Vases, bowls and flowerpots (Plate 34). Illustrated in a Burgess & Leigh catalogue of c1927 (Plate 33).

4002   Large open peony flowers and green leaves on a dark blue ground. Vases and bowls. Illustrated in a Burgess & Leigh catalogue of c1927 (Plate 33).

4009   Fruit and grapes design, tubed in brown and painted in pink, orange, fawn, blue and red-brown. Grey leaves. Fruit sets and suite ware.

4010   Lemons tubed in brown. Bowls and useful wares.

The following three designs for plaques were expensive to produce. They were probably tubed by Charlotte Rhead herself.

4011   Japanese female figure seated on a rug, perhaps after an unidentified Japanese print. Charlotte Rhead had previously used the same design at Wood's, with the image reversed and in a different colour arrangement (Fig 34).

4012   Pheasant perched in a tree and surrounded by pomegranates within a border of peaches. The design is known in several colour arrangements (Plate 39).

4013   Persian design of stylised flower-heads and elongated leaves within a border of scrolling devices and pointed leaves.

4014   Strawberries tubed in brown and painted in pink on a green ground. Bowls and useful wares.

4015   Bilberries tubed in brown and painted in blue and shades of purple on a green ground. Bowls and useful wares.

4016   Fruit design lustred in various colours on a white ground, the neck and base lustred in green or pink. Evidently a popular pattern, though the lustre is often found in poor condition. Bowls and vases (Plate 31).

Patterns 4070-4073 were probably designed in the summer of 1927.

4070   Open poppy flowers enamelled in pink, blue and orange with spiky centres. The design appears on bowls with embossed leaves painted in light and dark green.

4071   Plums in shades of purple, circular fruits and black grapes on bowls with embossed leaves in light and dark green (Plate 32).

4073   Cherries and small leaves painted in pink, purple and light green on bowls with embossed leaves in light and dark green.

4100   *Sylvan* Band of trees against a mountain range background. Probably adapted from a printed pattern (no. 3961) and designed in late 1927, it remained in production with several colour combinations, for over two years. Later produced in brighter colours with a gold finish (no. 4123). Vases and bowls (Plates 30 and 35).

4101   *Garland* Garlands of leaves and apples tubed in black on a white ground between light blue bands. Also produced in different colours (Plate 37).

The following sandwich sets (patterns 4102-4106) were made with a distinctive fan-shape dish and triangular plates (Plate 36). They were referred to as 'new' in The Pottery Gazette for Sept. 1928 (p.1415) which also drew attention to the Garland pattern (no. 4101) and its colour variations, nos.4104 and 4105.

4102   Fruits tubed in brown and painted in orange, fawn, purple and green. Reportedly known in other colours (Plate 38).

4103   Basket of fruits, painted in orange, fawn, pink, puce and green.

4104   Similar to no. 4101 (*Garland*), but painted in blue and red or blue and orange.

4105   Similar to no. 4101 (*Garland*), but painted in orange, fawn and green (Plate 36).

4106   Clusters of circular fruits (cherries?) on stems with leaves tubed in brown and painted in orange, fawn, pink, puce, purple and green.

4107   Seeded fruits and bunches of grapes on leafy stems painted in puce, blue, yellow and two shades of green. Bowls.

4108   *Florentine.* Various fruits and leaves on a dark blue ground; slip-stained cream body. Several examples of this pattern were kept in Burgess & Leigh's London showroom until the outbreak of World War Two. Vases, bowls, rose bowls, jardinières (Fig 38), tea and coffee sets. The name *Florentine* was later applied to a different pattern (no. 4752).

4109   Tomato design. Embossed bowls.

4110   As for no. 4000 but finished in orange lustre and black. Tea ware.

4111   Plaque decorated with a young woman in profile, richly dressed, holding a bunch of grapes in front of a parrot (Plate 44). The pattern, probably tubed by Charlotte Rhead herself, closely follows a painted design of 1921 by Louis Swettenham for Burgess & Leigh. Swettenham had previously worked for the firms of Minton and Doulton.

4111A. Similar to no. 4111, but with crimson lustred edge.

4112   *Persian.* "Persian" leaves tubed in black and painted in various colours. Lustred yellow inside and out. Bowls and vases.

4113	*Vine.* Fruiting vine design tubed in black and painted in various colours. Applied to embossed and other bowls (Plate 32).
4114	*Cretonne.* Flowers and fruits on leafy stems, tubed in black and finished in various coloured lustres. Bowls and vases.
4115	*Blossom.* Leaf and blossom design in various colours, tubed in black. Bowls and vases.
4116	*Aster.* Band of aster flowers in purple, blue and green tubed in black. Bowls and vases (Plate 42).
4117	Variation of *Persian* (no. 4112). Small bowls.
4118	Plaques decorated with a sailing boat on a swirling sea within a chequered border, all tubed in black (Plate 38).
4119	Variation of *Persian* (no. 4112).
4120	*Carnival.* Large stylised open flower design tubed in black and enamelled in red, coral, yellow and black (Plate 40). Bowls, vases, coffee cans and saucers. In production in 1929.
4121	Variation of *Carnival* (no. 4120) on a blue ground.
4123	*New Sylvan.* Variation of *Sylvan* (no. 4100). Finished in brighter colours with liquid gold embellishments.
4124	*New Garland.* Variation of *Garland* finished in orange and yellow lustres.
4125	*Berries.* Berries tubed in brown and painted underglaze in blue, purple and light green.
4126	Variation of *Berries* (no. 4125), painted underglaze in puce and purple.
4127	Variation of *Berries* (no. 4125), enamelled onglaze in yellow and orange.
4128	Stylised design, flower heads, multicoloured leaves and berries, tubed in black and enamelled in pink, yellow, blue and green. Fruit sets.
4129	Variation of 4128 enamelled in red, blue, yellow and green.
4131	Spray design enamelled in bright colours; composition not known. Bowls and vases.
4132	*Harlequin.* Stylised triangular shapes, each in the form of a harlequin's hat, enamelled in red, blue and green. Sandwich and fruit sets.
4133	*New Jazz.* Red stylised flower heads, blue and orange leaves with sprigs of multicoloured berries on a white ground. The design closely resembles no. 4128 of which it appears to be a variation. Sandwich and fruit sets.
4134	*Balloons.* Composition not known. Fruit sets.
4135	Scroll Panel Composition not known. Fruit sets.
4334	*Red Sunflower.* Red and orange petalled sunflowers with blue centres. Sandwich sets.
4335	*Blue Sunflower.* Composition not known; possibly blue petalled sunflowers with red centres. Sandwich sets.
4336	Fruit sprays with blue and gold finish. Sandwich sets.
4337	Fruit sprays with sunset red and black finish. Sandwich sets.
4338	Scroll design, tubed in black and enamelled in red and green. Bulb bowls.
4339	Stylised flower heads, purple petals with blue centres on a yellow ground, within triangular panels bounded by green and blue bands. Red bands round rim and base. Tubed in black. Bulb bowls.
4340	Variation of no. 4339. Same enamel colours; flower heads blue only. Tubed in black. Bulb bowls.
4341	Variation of no. 4339 with flower heads extending over borders. Tubed in black. Bulb bowls.
4347	*New Vine.* Fruiting vines and other fruit, the grapes painted underglaze in blue and the leaves lustred in green (Plate 43) or purple. Described in the trade press as "perhaps the most striking of the art ware". Vases and bowls.
4348	Pomegranates, grapes and other fruits within bands of five lobed geometric figures in light and dark blue. Described as "with blue Italian ornament". Vases and bowls.
4349	Plaque decorated with a female head looking to the left, tubed in black.
4350	Plaque decorated with a female head looking to the right, tubed in black.
4356	*Rutland.* Central spray of fruit within a yellow rustic trellis, enamelled in yellow, green, coral and orange. Sandwich sets and tea ware (Fig 39).
4357	Posy of three flower-heads enamelled in royal blue, coral and orange and green leaves on looping stems. Sandwich sets.
4367	Variation of Rutland (no. 4356). Rustic border and trellis enamelled in blue. Suite ware (Plate 45).
4416	Bird design tubed in black and enamelled in scarlet, blue, yellow and green. Suite ware.

The following three patterns, for children's ware, were printed, though tubed versions are also reported to have been made.[3]

4419	Dogs. *Bow Wow.*
4420	Cats. *Pussy.*
4421	Chickens. *Chick Chick* – chick emerged from a broken egg.
4422	As for no. 4416 but coloured blue all over.
4423	The pattern book states that this is a Charlotte Rhead design but gives no description. Vases.
4426	Underglaze powder blue decoration, tube-lined and sponged blue and white. A 1930 press report described it as having "a beautiful effect . . . Ought to create an appeal in every section of the trade". Suite ware. Twenty-three separate items are listed, ranging from biscuit jars and tea and coffee pots to six types of vase.
4470	Wreath design painted in black, green and red. Sandwich sets.
4471	Central panel with stylised tulip head, tubed in black and painted in blue, pink, puce, green and orange (Plate 46). Suite ware, embracing a wide range of useful items including teapots in three sizes.
4472	*Iris.* Naturalistic iris flower and stem, tubed in black on a blue ground. Sandwich sets.
4473	Corner panels of tulip heads painted in blue, pink, puce, orange and green. Sandwich sets.
4474	Corner panels with a plaid design painted in red, black, orange and green. Finished in green. Sandwich sets.

4480	Red flowerpot design. Tea ware.
4487	
or 4497	Oval fruits painted in pink and yellow with blue leaves on a powder blue ground. Vases.
4507	Scroll design. Vases.
4567	Crossed sticks and large daisies enamelled in various colours. Suite ware. The tea and dinner sets were produced with a printed pattern while other items were tube-lined.
4587	Lustre ware with central tube-lined pattern.
4609	*Sunshine.* Suite ware which included a 54 piece dinner service. Simple design of tubed dashes grouped in threes with a tubed dashed border. Graduated yellow ground.
4615	*Red Flowers (Nasturtiums).* Small size bowls.
4616	*Landscape.* Small size bowls
4628	According to the pattern book: "Rhead underglaze painting on matt glaze patt. as small size bowl". Presumably the pattern was similar either to no. 4615 (*Nasturtiums*) or no. 4616 (*Landscape*). Suite ware.
4663	Blue vases and bowls, matt glaze, enamelled in red and finished in liquid gold.

The following patterns, nos.4672-4700A, were not tube-lined.

4672	Tigers and silver-lustred palm trees. Vases.
4678, 4678A–	As for no. 4672, but with colour variations. Vases.
4697	Sprays of berries printed in black and enamelled in coral. Includes bonbon trays with handles enamelled in coral, black and scoured gold.
4698	As for no. 4697, but bonbon trays with puce handles.
4700	Bird and leaf pattern printed onglaze, enamelled in green and coral and finished in scoured gold. Suite ware.
4700A	Similar to no. 4700. Bonbon trays with scoured gold handles.

The following patterns were the last to be designed by Charlotte Rhead for Burgess & Leigh. They were in production by the end of 1931

4752	*Florentine.* Curvilinear geometric design, lustred in dull green and brown or brown alone, with a mottled brown glaze (Plate 47). The commonest of Charlotte Rhead's designs for Burgess & Leigh, it remained in production for several years. Examples are known incorrectly marked 'Bennett'. Advertised in June 1932 as *Burleigh Florentine Ware* and available 'in an extensive range of vases and bowls'.
4753	Plaque decorated with a ship. Perhaps a variation of no. 4118.
4766	*Quack Quack.* Four ducks in a field. Another printed children's ware pattern (see nos. 4419, 4420 and 4421). It may also have been tubed.
4767	*Orchard.* Blue apples and green leaves tubed in blue. Described in the trade press in 1932 as 'a smart new pattern'. Suite ware.
4768	As for no. 4767, but with orange apples and green leaves tubed in black.
4789	*Laurel Band.* Band of brown laurel leaves on a blue ground; broken brown glaze (Plate 37). Vases.
4809	Band of sketchy stylised flower heads with spiralling outlines tubed in blue; finished with gold spirals; mottled brown glaze. Vases, bowls and flower jugs.
4809A	As for no. 4809, but no gold spirals.
4816	Variation of *Florentine* (no. 4752) with a broad central zigzag band above a band of leaf forms. Vases and bowls.
4831	As for no 4809, but with pink lustre finish and purple flower heads with silver spirals. Vases and bowls.
4832	As for no. 4809, but with yellow lustre finish and blue flower heads with silver spirals. Vases and bowls.
4833	Trellis pattern between bands of elongated leaves and scrolling foliage. The panels within the trellis enamelled in coral and black and the leaves semi-gilded. Vases and bowls.
4834	As for no. 4833, but with some panels lustred in green. Mottled brown glaze.
4908	*New Florentine.* Brown or green lustred sunbursts separated by blue bands, all within bands of brown diamond shapes. Mottled brown glaze. Vases and bowls. Apparently Charlotte Rhead's last design for Burgess & Leigh and probably produced after she had left the company.

Backstamps Burgess & Leigh Ltd.

Backstamp 1 – *c1926-1928.*	*Backstamp 2 –* *MADE IN ENGLAND* *beneath beehive* *c1928-1929.*	*Backstamp 3 –* *ENGLAND only* *beneath beehive* *c1928-1929.*	*Backstamp 4 –* *Mark used on some* *wares made for* *Lawleys' retail* *shops c1928-1929.*	*Backstamp 5 –* *smaller version* *of No. 3, c1931.*

CHAPTER SIX

A. G. Richardson (Crown Ducal)

Exactly when Charlotte Rhead joined A. G. Richardson, makers of Crown Ducal Ware, at the Gordon Pottery in Tunstall is uncertain. As her first designs for the company began to appear early in 1933, it may have been around the previous November. To judge from the report of a meeting of the Society of Industrial Artists held in Hanley on October 10th 1932[1] it seems unlikely that she was there in mid October. At that meeting Gordon Forsyth[2] gave a lecture entitled 'What is Modern Art?', though the talk was really about modern design in the Potteries. During the discussion that followed, one of Charlotte's uncles, Bertrand Rhead, argued that ' "modern art" had emanated from the Continent', and that it did not sell. Buyers wanted 'designs of a typical English nature, designed by Englishmen' and not what he described as 'tripe'. 'We have got in this room and in the Staffordshire Potteries a bunch of clever pottery designers, and I, for one, protest against the idea of men being introduced from London to teach us how to decorate pottery.'[3] Also present at the Forsyth lecture was one of the Richardson directors, Joseph Harrison, who pleaded not so much for modern art as for simplicity and good taste appropriate to the modern home. But, he enquired, 'Where could they turn for artists?', a question he repeated a little later, adding 'We are not designers . . . We have got the workpeople; better workers there are not to be found in the whole world. But where are the artists?'[4] These hardly seem to be the words of a man who had just engaged one of the best designers in the Potteries – as Charlotte Rhead must at that time have surely been considered. Burgess & Leigh had described her as 'the accomplished lady artist'[5] when she joined the company in 1926 and her work there, much acclaimed in the trade press, as the previous chapter made clear, had undoubtedly enhanced her reputation.

Whether or not Charlotte was herself at the meeting, it is tempting to think that, as a consequence, it was her uncle who subsequently introduced her to Joseph Harrison and to Richardson's. Although this must remain pure speculation it is not entirely unlikely as Bertrand Rhead, according to his daughter Marjorie Wood, was a friend of the Harrison family.

Whatever the circumstances which led to Charlotte's arrival at Richardson's, the company had not made use of the tube-lined technique before and no doubt her reputation as the leading designer of this type of ware played some part in her appointment. The company already had an established art director, W. B. Johnson, who had been with the firm since 1917, but his work appears to have been fairly conventional, consisting for the most part of run-of-the-mill floral designs. Although he did not retire until 1937, he worked mainly as the decorating shop manager at the Gordon Pottery.

Rather oddly, Charlotte's position at Richardson's never seems to have been clearly defined, nor has it been possible to assign any specific post in the company to her. She was undoubtedly involved in one way or another with many of the company's activities though it was her tube-lined designs, coupled with her use of mottled glazes, which seem to have made an immediate impact on Richardson's fortunes. One of the earliest of these designs, *Byzantine* (Plate 48), first mentioned in the trade press in March 1933, was so successful that it remained in production for some years, appearing in several colour arrangements and under various names. Soon she was also working on tableware, and another early production was a range which had a 'stitched' raised border, the 'stitches', a series of parallel dashes, being tubed in two colours, or in black alone. Despite the recession, the pattern sold extremely well, and continued to do so for several years. It is said that she derived the idea from the stitching which appeared on the lapels of the more expensive men's suits – thus, by implication, giving the tableware an up-market appearance.[6] These achievements were all the more remarkable as at about this time her father Frederick Alfred had became terminally ill, dying not long after the appearance of the *Byzantine* pattern.

Richardson's had strong links with the United States through its New York agents, Maddock & Miller. As Crown Ducal products were of good quality and reasonably priced, Charlotte Rhead's inspired designing enabled the company to weather the Depression and even to expand. In 1933 a second pottery, the Britannia in Cobridge, was acquired, mainly for the production of tableware. This was at a time when many other companies were in financial difficulties; even William Moorcroft, one of Britain's most prestigious potters, whose tube-lined productions were sought by collectors and museums worldwide, was forced to put his staff on part-time. In one respect Moorcroft's difficulties turned to Charlotte's advantage, as she was able to engage Fanny Morrey as her senior tube-liner. Fanny was a decorator of great experience, having worked for Moorcroft since about 1900, and her arrival at Richardson's during a period of expansion must have been of considerable help to Charlotte. It was to her that Charlotte entrusted the tubing of many of her new and experimental designs. She also permitted Fanny to use 'L. Rhead' when marking her wares, while insisting that the other tube-liners used the more formal 'C. Rhead'. With her enhanced status she was now 'Charlotte' to the world rather than the familiar 'Lottie' which had been used at Ellgreave and Burgess & Leigh.

For the tube-lined wares, Charlotte preferred to use stylised fruit and flower designs such as *Byzantine* , although naturalistic designs also made their appearance. One of the earliest of these, *Primula* (Plate 49), may have been based on a drawing by her uncle, George Woolliscroft Rhead, who published several books on design[7], or from her own close observation of plant forms. As has been said, *Byzantine* was made in several colour combinations, some of which were given foreign-sounding names such as *Persino* (Plate 54). The pattern proved so popular that it was even applied to utility wares, plates, teapots, coffee pots, and cups and saucers (Plate 48). Another popular stylised floral pattern, *Persian Rose* (Plate 65), designed two years later, was also made in several colours and with different glazes. Rather illogically, around 1934, all these variations seem to have been renamed *Tudor Rose*.

Despite the depressed financial climate, the company went ahead with the works necessary for adapting the newly acquired Britannia Pottery to its particular needs. These must have taken some time but by the summer of 1934 production there was up and running and by September Richardson's was able to announce that 'in order to facilitate deliveries and to meet the increased demand for their productions, they have reopened the Britannia Pottery, Cobridge'.[8] This 'increased demand' must have been due in large measure to Charlotte's flair for producing successful designs and she now divided her time between the Gordon Pottery, where the tube-lining was carried out, and the Britannia, where she had charge of the freehand paint shop.

About the time Richardson's were adapting the Britannia, Charlotte and her mother were moving home. After her father's death in 1933 they left the house in Marsh Avenue, Wolstanton where they had lived for many years and rented a small property in Stoneleigh Road, Tunstall. This move may have been made for convenience as the house was near the Gordon Pottery. By now Charlotte was driving to work in a small car she had bought as transport of some kind became necessary to facilitate travel between the two Richardson potteries.

While living in Tunstall she took up copper-plate engraving, an evening occupation which she usually undertook on the kitchen table. Perhaps Charlotte's inspiration for this activity came from her uncle, George Woolliscroft Rhead, who had learned the skill from the French artist Alphonse Legros when a student at the South Kensington School of Art in the 1870s. A fluent and prolific artist, among his many works were a series of etchings specially commissioned by Wedgwood's (Fig. 2). Charlotte was now working on tableware designs for Richardson's, and made prints of some of them to send to her brother, Frederick Hurten Rhead, in America. On one floral pattern, *Dell*, she noted in manuscript 'I etched the complete service of this', and on another pattern 'I etched service of this – but was a very trying job – so fine'.[9]

Like other members of her family, Charlotte took great interest in the decorative effects of glazes and lustres. An appropriate finish was, for her, an essential part of the overall design. Lustres were very fashionable during the thirties as indeed they had been in the 1920s when she was working with her father at Wood's. They suited the contemporary style of decoration and Charlotte frequently used them, sometimes in conjunction with touches of on-glaze enamels. A good example of this combination of techniques is provided by her well-known *Golden Leaves* pattern (Plates 67, 72). Though she was not a chemist, she devised a number of new glazes using commercial mixtures, including several so-called 'broken' glazes which produced an attractive mottled effect. These mottled glazes were very successful and were an innovation for Richardson's. But perhaps her most unusual glaze, which was applied to both tableware and decorative items, appeared around 1936. This 'snow glaze', as it was called, produced a thick and irregular white matt finish, described by a trade journal at the time as 'resembling a layer of freshly-fallen snow flakes'.[10] It created something of a sensation in the Potteries, and as the trade journal went on to observe, 'We understand that the demand for this new type of decoration outstrips all anticipation'.[11] It seems to have been equally popular in the United States, Maddock and Miller claiming in an advertisement that 'it presents a surface that is thick and velvety to the touch – permits subtle color effects in underglaze decorations'. It was probably snow glaze tableware that Frederick Hurten Rhead saw in a shop in Pittsburgh in December 1936, as he noted, though without comment, in his day-book at the time.[12]

Charlotte Rhead used the snow glaze to add variety to several of her existing tube-lined patterns, including a fresh version of *Tudor Rose*, the white

Fig 40 The Crown Ducal display at the British Industries Fair, 1937. The Foxglove (no. 4953) and Wisteria (no. 4954) patterns on the central stand dominate the exhibit.

ground spectacularly setting off the flowers which were enamelled in black and gold (Plate 65). Some new naturalistic designs also appeared with a snow glaze ground, among them the popular *Foxglove* and *Wisteria* patterns (Plates 76 & 77), these two designs forming the centrepiece for the large Richardson display at the 1937 British Industries Fair (Fig 40). The snow glaze was also used for the wares specially produced that year for the coronation of George VI and Queen Elizabeth, the present Queen Mother. In addition to the standard commemorative pieces, plaques, vases and many other shape in three different colour arrangements (Plate 70), they included a range of comports. These were decorated with photographs of Princess Elizabeth – later Queen Elizabeth II – and Princess Margaret, taken by Vandyk, the court photographer. They were much admired by their grandmother, Queen Mary.

Some of the snow glaze tableware produced at the time by Richardson's can be attributed to Charlotte. The handled bottle illustrated in Plate 63 is probably hers as well. This simple but elegant design is not tube-lined, but carved in the clay and painted underglaze in three colours, the carved dashed edges being a typical decorative device of hers. One of her most abstract designs in the modern style, again using a snow glaze, may have been an experimental piece (Fig 41). W. B. Johnson was still the titular art director at the time, but it seems unlikely that he made much use of this new glaze and, in any case, was on the point of retirement. Some contemporary snow glaze designs may have been by other hands, possibly the work of young trainee designers. Charlotte had several trainees over whom she no doubt kept a close eye. Besides these various activities, Charlotte also had a say in developing new shapes, or so it would appear from a 1936 Richardson's advertisement. Alongside an illustration of some of her work, it referred to 'new shapes and designs in flower jugs, vases and bowls by Charlotte Rhead'.[13]

Fig 41 "Modern" design by Charlotte Rhead. Probably a trial piece.

Early in 1937 Richardson's New Zealand agent visited the Potteries. He was impressed with Charlotte's designs which he felt had not been sufficiently appreciated in his country and undertook to launch a major advertising campaign on his return to Wellington.[14] He may have been successful, as examples of Crown Ducal tube-lined wares turn up in that country quite frequently. He was followed by a representative of the New York firm of Maddock and Miller, and Charlotte was reported to be 'busy getting samples ready for him'.[15] These would undoubtedly have included some of her tableware designs which the company was active in promoting in the United States.

Three months later there were more American visitors, Charlotte's elder brother, Frederick Hurten Rhead and his third wife Winifred, and her other brother, Harry, and his wife, Sally. Frederick Hurten was now a major figure in the United States ceramics world, chairman of the Arts and Designs Committee of the United States Potters Association and the art director of the Homer Laughlin China Company of Newell, West Virginia. He had recently introduced a new range of tableware, *Fiesta Ware*, which was having an extraordinary success in the United States, so his visit aroused considerable interest in the Potteries. On the 8th of June, in Hanley Town Hall, he addressed a crowded meeting of the North Staffordshire Branch of the Society of Industrial Artists on 'Mass Production in American Potteries'. In his long talk, he stressed the need for the pottery industry to employ competent designers with a background in ceramics – a favourite theme of his. "It is my conviction," he said, "that the successful decorative man . . . is the one who functions as 90% organisation man and 10% artist".[16] Frederick would certainly have included Charlotte in his description for he knew that his sister was a thoroughgoing commercial potter who would loyally devote herself to any organisation for which she worked.

If Frederick was thinking of Charlotte at this time, he must also have been worried about her too, for during his visit she had been diagnosed as having breast cancer which required immediate surgery. Frederick had to return to the United States at the end of June, but her other brother Harry[17] and Sally remained. This must have comforted Charlotte as they were able to take her home after the operation and before their return to Zanesville. But as her sister Dollie observed in a letter to Frederick, 'It is going to take her some time to pick up as it has been a big thing, but had to be done. She has been very plucky and I hope she can keep her pecker up after Harry and Sally go'.[18]

On the face of it Charlotte seems to have recovered well and some months later decided to buy a house in Watlands Avenue, Wolstanton, to which she and her mother moved from Tunstall. About this time the tube-lining shop was transferred from the Gordon Pottery to the Britannia, partly no doubt because of the better facilities there, but also perhaps for reasons of economy. For the Potteries were once again in a period of recession, with many employees being placed on part-time. But now Charlotte's creative flair was unable to reverse the trend, as it had done so successfully five years before. Rather it showed signs of flagging as her designs became more stereotyped. In spite of appearances, this must in part have been due to the cancer.

The outbreak of World War Two in 1939 brought new worries, professional and personal. Many of the experienced staff left Richardson's, often to go into the better paid munitions industry. There were changes in Richardson's management, too, and the new conditions severely restricted output. The fall of France in 1940 cut her off from her younger sister Katherine (Sister St. Pierre). She had become a nun in the 1920s, joining the Ursulines, a French teaching order which had its headquarters in Dole in the Jura. This order ran an important school in Versailles where Katherine was working when the Germans occupied Paris. She was arrested and subsequently interned with other British female nationals in Clermont-Ferrand. Meanwhile, their brother Frederick Hurten had also developed cancer and died in a hospital in New York City at the end of 1942. Before that, sometime towards the end of 1941 or early in 1942, she and Richardson's had parted company in circumstances that are unclear.[19] It must have been an unsatisfactory end to what had been a fruitful relationship.

Richardson's revived the production of tube-lined wares after the war, perhaps as a result of observing the success of a new range which Charlotte had devised for the firm of H. J. Wood Ltd. which she had joined after leaving Richardson's. Several of her 1930s designs reappeared, sometimes with different colourings, and Richardson's also developed and marketed some new patterns. Though these sometimes incorporate Charlotte's motifs, they lack the crispness and the overall balance of her compositions. Moreover these post-war productions are often very poorly decorated – the kind of work she would not have tolerated from her tube-liners. Their quality apart, rising costs and a punitive rate of purchase tax made it difficult to market tube-lined wares at popular prices, though production did continue until at least 1962.

The Gordon Pottery was closed during the war and in 1974 the company sold the Britannia Pottery to Enoch Wedgwood (Tunstall) Ltd. This firm has now gone out of business and the building has been converted to other uses.

Notes for Collectors
The list of patterns that follows is based on the Richardson pattern books, most of which have recently become available. While not complete, they do provide a comprehensive and accurate guide to the patterns Charlotte Rhead designed for the company between the latter part of 1933 and the early years of World War Two. At the same time they show that at Richardson's, as at other potteries, the system relating patterns and numbers was not invariably adhered to. So collectors should not expect absolute certainties.

During the time she worked for Richardson's, Charlotte Rhead's more elaborate decorative tube-lined pieces were usually marked on their bases with her facsimile signature. This signature was added by the tube-liner who carried out the tubed decoration on the piece, though the signature was sometimes omitted. If the tube-liners were paid on a piecework basis, they might not wish to spend the time on this additional embellishment. Again, in order to speed production of a popular pattern, management might decide that work on each piece should be completed as quickly as possible. This may have been the case with *Golden Leaves* (no. 4921) as so many examples of this popular pattern seem to lack a signature, though some of these signature-less works must belong to the period when the pattern was revived in 1951. The post-war productions, which include a number of Charlotte's 1930s patterns, would not have carried a facsimile signature as Charlotte Rhead had died in 1946, and in any case she had severed her links with the company in 1941 or 1942.

Apart from these decorative works, many more of Charlotte's designs in the 1930s did not carry a facsimile signature. These included the less important and simpler designs, such as *Stitch* and *Patch* (Plate 50), her tableware, her many painted patterns and the tubed nursery ware.

Some collectors attach great importance to this signature, and marked pieces are usually more expensive than those that are not. In fact the signature, not being Charlotte's own, has no real significance if the design is known to be hers. So collectors may do better to buy unmarked pieces – they will usually get more for their money. A point to note is that most facsimile signatures on Richardson pieces use the initial "C" (for Charlotte) instead of the "L" (for Lottie, her familiar name, adopted by her family and close friends) which had been used at Burgess & Leigh. Nevertheless the "L" does sometime appear, notably on work decorated by the senior tube-liner, Fanny Morrey.

Apart from the facsimile signature, the bases of the Richardson productions usually carry several other marks. Almost invariably there is a printed Crown Ducal backstamp. Over the years Richardson's used several different backstamps and examples, with approximate dates, are illustrated at the end of this chapter. In addition there may be a tube-liner's identification mark (on the more elaborate tube-lined wares only), some of which are given below, and a separate decorator's mark, added by the lustrer or paintress concerned. There may also be a two- or three-figure shape number which may be impressed, tubed or painted, or occasionally both tubed and painted.

Lastly, there may be a tubed or painted four-figure pattern number. Such numbers are most useful to collectors as they are a valuable aid to identification though they too have to be treated with some caution. Painted numbers, for instance, can be difficult to read and although tubed numbers are usually clearer, they are not always correct. Thus the *Florian* pattern plaque illustrated in Plate 71 is plainly marked in tube-line with the number 4971 – and by the senior tube-liner Fanny Morrey at that – though the true number should be 4922. While such errors are not particularly common, this is by no means an isolated example. The *Fruit Border* plaque in Plate 82 is wrongly tubed with 4921, the *Golden Leaves* pattern number, and a piece with the *Persian Leaf* design is known with an incorrectly tubed pattern number overpainted with a new number which is also wrong.

Not all the names of these tube-liners are known, so the list that follows and the collated tube-liner's marks is incomplete. As for the lustrers and painters, many different marks, the majority of them numbers, have been observed. The sheer quantity reflects the substantial size of the staff employed in the decorating shops at one time or another in the 1930s. As most of these decorators remain anonymous, no attempt to list them has been attempted.

Despite the emergence of the pattern books, the descriptions of the patterns that follow is incomplete. The book containing Charlotte Rhead's earliest patterns for Richardson's is still missing and must be presumed lost while the last book is dilapidated. In the books that have come to light some patterns are named while others are not. There are particular problems too with patterns of a similar design but decorated with different colours as there was no consistency of treatment. Some have different numbers, others have no number and in other cases again the same number was used despite the colour changes. For some patterns, the same name was retained despite colour changes while for others these changes involved a name change too. A notable example is the popular *Persian Rose* pattern (no. 4040) which occurs in a variety of colour arrangements and with different glazes, all of which appear to have been named *Tudor Rose*. It is hard to discern the logic behind this arrangement.

In addition to the established designs which occur without pattern numbers, less familiar numberless works also turn up from time to time. Some of these may be samples, made for the Richardson travellers to try out "on the road". If they were not successful there, or if they proved to be too expensive to manufacture, they did not go into production. As a general rule, these rejected samples were evidently not entered in the pattern books and so do not appear in the list that follows. Even this does not appear to have been a practice universally followed though, as the pattern books do include some designs which are known not to have been manufactured in any quantity.

As already indicated, some patterns were given names as well as numbers and where these are known, they are included. Other names listed in the trade press have not so far been identified and a few may even have been devised by the press itself.

Confusingly, the Richardson's staff sometimes used names for certain patterns which differ from the pattern book names. The popular *Golden Leaves* (Plates 67, 72) again provides a good example, having apparently been known to many of the decorators at the time as *Falling Leaves*. This last was the title when Richardson's revived it again in 1951.

A. G. Richardson Decorators
Tube-liners and their marks
A   Adams?
B   Violet Barber?
)   Rose Dickenson (Mrs Cumberbatch)
F   Fanny Morrey
H   Hannah Williams
J   Dora Jones
.K.   Katie Wall or Lily Kidd?
L.   Lily Eardley or Lily Kidd?
M   Minnie Walker
R   Mabel Rowley
I   ?
2   Elsie Fearns?
111   Marjorie Windsor?

A. G. Richardson Crown Ducal Tube-lined Patterns
Pattern names marked * are those suggested to the writer by contemporary trade press reports. The remainder are taken from the A. G. Richardson pattern and other record books.

2607   Stylised orange and yellow flowers with spiky petals between yellow stylised leaves and small blue stylised flower heads with red centres. No border.
2681   *Byzantine* As for no. 2607 but within a banded and hatched border. First mentioned in the trade press in March 1933. A popular pattern (Plate 48), in production for a number of years in several colour arrangements.
2682   Brown lotus leaves overlaid with a zigzag band of thin spiky leaves. The mottled ground may be brown or green (Plate 49).
2691   *Turin* Bands of overlapping lotus leaves with thin lines running down from the apex of each leaf. Produced in various colour combinations including greens, blues and browns. Despite the Italian name, the pattern appears to have been developed from a K'ang Hsi design (Plates 51 and 117).
2693   Perhaps similar to no. 2682.
2800   Geometric design with alternating red and black stepped forms. Mottled orange ground. Probably inspired by contemporary interest in Aztec architecture (Plate 57).
2801   As for *Byzantine* (no. 2681) but with cerise and purple flowers (Plate 48).

[Number not known] *Primula* Naturalistic flowering primroses on a pale green ground. Mentioned in the trade press in February 1934 (Plate 49).

2979   Lemonade jug tubed with "Another little drink wont do us any harm" in black. Black tubed stitching round mouth.
2980   As for no. 2979 but smaller sized jug.
2981   Lemonade jug tubed in brown with "Another little drink wont do us any harm".
2982   Mug tubed in black with "Another little drink wont do us any harm".
2983   As for no. 2982 but tubed in brown.
2984   As for no. 2980 but tubed in brown.
2985   Mug tubed in black with "Show me the way to go home".
2986   Mug tubed with "Another little drink wont do us any harm". Cross hatched and stitched handle.

The next four patterns were for Cotswold shape tableware. These were undecorated apart from stitched edgings designed by Charlotte Rhead. These edgings were tubed in various colours, normally by juniors or apprentices, though some larger plaques were evidently worked by the senior tube-liners (see no. 3049).

3048	Stitched edge. Orange.
3049	Stitched edge. Orange and black alternately. A large plaque (d.44 cm.) is known in this pattern tubed by Dora Jones and with a Rhead facsimile signature. This may have been one of the 'matching trays' which, together with 'the extra large size salad bowls', were intended for the North American market (see no. 3218 and note 20).
3050	Stitched edge. Crimson underglaze.
3051	Stitched edge. Black and crimson alternately.
3052	*Persino* As for *Byzantine* (no. 2681) but with bright green glaze (Plate 54).

The following seven patterns were for tube-lined Nursery Ware. They are usually found marked only with a Crown Ducal backstamp.

3131	*Who said dinner?* Yellow chick in a field with tufts of grass and two blue flowers (Plate 53).
3132	*Is it carrots?* Squatting rabbit eating a carrot (Plate 115).
3133	*Little Boy Blue* (Plate 53).
3134	*Tom the Piper's son* Running boy with a pig under his arm.
3135	*Red Riding Hood*

Two other subjects are known though they do not appear to have been given pattern numbers.

Polly put the kettle on (Plate 53).

Poodles Two poodle dogs. The same design also appears with the title *Fi Fi*.

3169	Central tree design tubed in black and orange with a similarly coloured dashed edge.
3170	Dragon design tubed in black and orange with a similarly coloured dashed edge. The pattern may only have been used for large bowls and matching trays (see note 20). The dragon design reappeared in pattern no. 4511.
3191	Galleon tubed in matt blue on a white ground. The ship, with the design reversed, appears to have been adapted from the source used for Burgess & Leigh pattern 4118 (Plate 38).
3205	Running laurel leaf border tubed in matt blue between tubed blue spots.
3218	*Blossom* Central spray of flowers and leaves tubed in two blues with a blue tubed running laurel leaf border (no. 3205). This and the related *Blossom* designs, appear to have been applied mainly to large salad bowls and matching supper trays for the United States market.[20]
3257	*Blossom* Identical design to no. 3218.
3257B	*Blossom* Similar to nos. 3218 and 3257 but within a blue stitch border.
3258	*Blossom* Central spray of flowers and leaves as nos. 3218 and 3257, but tubed in orange and black within an orange and black stitch border.
3259	Central tree design tubed in orange and black; identical to no. 3169.
3260	*Florentine* Central spray of three flower-heads on stems with spiky leaves and tubed in two blues within a dashed two-blue border and a rustic undulating blue band (perhaps table-ware only).
3272	*Rhodian* Stylised flower-heads enamelled in scarlet, orange, yellow, gold, black and grey; uncoloured leaves; mottled beige glaze. Tubed in black. Mentioned in the trade press in 1934 and 1935 (Plate 56). Also known with leaves lustred in silver, or with blue flowers and leaves lustred in green (Plate 103).
3273	Bands of blue, orange and mauve on a ribbon design outlined with black tubed dots. Mottled fawn underglaze ground under yellow lustre.
3274	*Stitch** Vertical stripes enamelled in scarlet, black and orange within a black dotted outline, lustred orange and yellow on a thin mottled ground. A very popular pattern, usually worked by apprentice tube-liners and juniors. Never marked with a Rhead facsimile signature. Also produced in other colours and in several variations from 1934 onwards (Plate 50).
3321	*Granada* Large red pomegranates and leaves tubed in blue. Enamelled in pink, blue, green, brown and mauve and lustred. Introduced in late 1933 (Plates 49 and 107)).
3370	Central spray of three flower-heads tubed in two shades of blue. Similar to no. 3260.
3375	Central flower spray and leaves tubed in two blues and similar to 3218 and 3257, but within a dashed light and dark blue border and a blue running rustic band.
3505	*Stitch** As for no. 3274 (Plate 50), but applied to a 'lamp vase'. Solid black rim and base.
3506	As for no. 3505 with black tubed stitch decoration; solid black bands top and bottom. White matt mottled ground. Alternate panels and top lustred in orange.
3507	As for no. 3506, but green lustre bands top and bottom and alternate panels on side in yellow lustre.
3509	Lamp vase' decorated with the *Turin* pattern (no. 2691). Enamelled in orange, gold and grey.
3514	As for no. 2691, but enamelled in orange, black and brown. Green glaze.
3636	*Padua* As for no. 2691, but the lower parts of the overlapping leaves in orange. Brown mottled glaze.
3637	*Padua* As for no. 2691, but the lower parts of the overlapping leaves in black, outlined in scarlet and orange. Grey mottled glaze (Plate 52).
3639	*Byzantine* As for no. 2681, but flowers enamelled in blue, pink and mauve. Green leaves. Ground not mottled. Straw glaze. This variation may have been applied mainly to large bowls and trays (see note 20).

3727	Blue enamelled trailing leaf design on a blue mottled ground with narrow gold bands (Plate 62). Also produced in green (no. 4050) and pink (no. 5728). In later variations the leaves were tubed (nos. 6568 and 6668).
3729	*Azalia* (sic). Tube-lined in blue. Grey glaze. The pattern appears to resemble no. 4016.
3797	*Hydrangea* Clusters of pink and mauve hydrangea flowers on brown leafy stems tubed in blue. Brown mottled glaze. Introduced at the British Industries Fair in February 1935 (Plate 55). A similar printed design was used for tableware.
4015	*Patch** A development of *Stitch** (no. 3274). Patchwork effect, the patches being 'stitched' to the body of the piece in Danube blue tube-line and enamelled in lemon yellow, orange and two shades of green. Grey mottled glaze. Like *Stitch** this design was worked by the juniors and was never marked with a Rhead facsimile signature.
4016	*Blue Peony** Stylised blue and puce peony flowers with spiky puce and blue leaves, tubed in blue. Also known with blue and pink leaves. Grey mottled glaze. Introduced in 1935 (Plate 58).
4017	*Patch** As for no. 4015, but tubed in black stitch and enamelled in scarlet, black and orange.
4036	*Omar* Persian male figure seated under a tree in a rocky landscape. Beside him is a cloth on which stands a flask, a jug and a loaf of bread, with the tube-lined inscription 'Here with a loaf of bread beneath the bough A flask of wine A book of verse and Thou'.[21] On vases, in addition a deity emerges from the clouds. Edged with blue and red dots and a green line. Fawn glaze. Tubed in black. Shown at the British Industries Fair in February 1935 (Plate 59).
4038	*Omar* As for no. 4036, but blue and green dot edge. Blue glaze.
4040	*Persian Rose* Stylised rose-heads with a double row of petals and cross-hatched and striped centres, enamelled in pink, orange, scarlet and blue. Green leaves and multi-coloured berries. Mottled grey glaze. The design was also produced in several other colour arrangements (nos. 4300, 4318, 4479, 4491, and 5393). All these variations appear to have been named *Tudor Rose*. The pattern was revived in 1951. A variation, no pattern number and perhaps a trial, has blue flowers, green leaves and blue and yellow berries, all enclosed within yellow bands. Plates 64, 65, & 102.
4050	Enamelled green and orange trailing leaf design; variation of no. 3727. Banded in copper. Mottled fawn ground aerographed over in grey.
4088	Variation of *Patch** (no. 4015). Unlike nos.4015 and 4018, the patches on this version were lustred and not enamelled. According to the pattern book these lustre colours were primrose, green, black and orange, the tube-lined stitching was black and the glaze was mottled fawn (Plate 50). In practice, there were a number of colour variations in the individual patches, the green, for instance, sometimes being replaced by brown. Shown at the British Industries Fair in February 1935 where it was much admired.[22]
4098	Variation of *Florentine* (no. 3260). Tubed in black and enamelled in orange and blue.
4100	Band of interlinked off-white 'commas' enclosing shapes lustred alternately in orange and black (Plate 61). Introduced in 1935. The pattern also appears with different colour arrangements (nos.4298 and 4968). Other variations, without pattern numbers, include an overall covering of blue lustre, with yellow and pink lustred 'commas' tubed in brown.
4298	As for no. 4100, but coloured in silver and green. Tubed in black. Off-white ground. This pattern was revived after World War Two.
4300	*Tudor Rose* As for *Persian Rose* (no. 4040) but with puce and blue flowers, grey lustre leaves. Snow glaze (Plate 64).
4318	*Tudor Rose* As for *Persian Rose* (no. 4040) but with orange and primrose lustred flowers and grey lustred leaves. Tubed in black. Snow glaze. On some examples the leaves are dark grey in colour (Plate 65).
4328	Green Dragon centre. The pattern book gives no other details. This design may not have been executed.
4479	*Tudor Rose* As for *Persian Rose* (no. 4040), but with the inner petals lustred in orange and the outer petals glazed off-white. Leaves lustred in light and dark brown. Tubed in brown.
4491	*Tudor Rose* As for *Persian Rose* (no. 4040), but with lustred orange and fawn glazed flowers and leaves lustred in light and dark brown. In this design, which resembles no. 4479, roses with outer petals lustred in orange alternate with flowers in which the inner petals only are lustred. Shown at the 1936 British Industries Fair (Plate 65).
4511	*Green Dragon*, generally known as *Manchu*. Chinese dragon, in green with brown hair and tail and finished in gold, surrounded by cloud scrolls and other devices. Mottled off-green glaze (Plate 68). There is also an uncoloured version. The original design, tubed by Charlotte Rhead herself, was in brown (Plate 60). The pattern was revived in 1951.
4516	Central rampant lion tubed in black surrounded by four-petalled stylised flower heads and clover leaf forms within a border of scarlet and black geometric shapes. Snow glaze.
4517	*Blossom* Central spray of flowers as no. 3258 but tubed in blue within a border of flower-heads grouped in threes and connected by a running band of stems and leaves all tubed in blue. Snow glaze.
4518	Design carved in the clay. Band of irregular oval shapes and dashed lines painted underglaze in copper green, blue and yellow. Snow glaze. Although not tubed, this decorative design can be attributed to Charlotte Rhead on stylistic grounds (Plate 63).
4519	Stylised flowers with angular zig-zag petals enamelled in scarlet, orange, yellow and blue. Green stems and leaves. Tubed in brown. A simple design, presumably intended to sell for a low price.
4520	A variation of the *Stitch** design. Four interlocking lobed shapes enamelled in blue, yellow, green and scarlet. Stitched surround and rim. Green bands top and bottom.

4521	Tubed sprays of four-petalled flower heads enamelled in blues, pink, purple green and orange. Green stems and leaves, all within blue bands with blue stitching (Plate 69). The colours of the flower-heads may vary.
4523	See no. 4538.
4528	As for no. 4521, but flowers lustred in yellow and orange with black lustre centres and stems. No stitch on top.
4529	As for no. 4521, but flowers enamelled in scarlet, orange and black. Brown lustre band on top but no stitch. Orange lustre inside.
4530	As for no. 4529, but orange lustre band at top. Broad lustre foot band.
4531	As for no. 4530, but brown lustre.
4532	As for no. 4520, but within a narrow blue edge.
4533	Same design as no. 4520, but enamelled in blue, yellow and scarlet only. Tubed in brown. Thin blue and green bands.
4534	Tubed or painted design. Broad central band with a running stem from which project groups of three circular orange and brown fruits alternating with triplets of green leaves Mottled grey glaze.
4536	Stylized lily buds in profile, tubed in brown and enamelled in orange, yellow and green. Snow glaze.
4536A	As for no. 4536 but enamelled in two shades of green and different shades of orange and yellow.
4536B	As for no. 4536 but enamelled in blue, green, pink, yellow and puce.
4538	*Blossom* Plaques, vases etc. Snow glaze. Pattern identical to no. 4517, but sold at British Industries Fair as no. 4523.
4619	As for no. 4521 but without blue stitching.
4622	*Stitch** variation. One line of stitching above and around pattern only. Central band lustred in primrose, top and bottom lustred in orange.
4724	*Coronation Ware* Snow glaze ground decorated with a chequer pattern of orange and white squares and the Royal Cypher. The white squares have black dots in their centres. Tubed in black. Designed in 1936 for the projected coronation of Edward VIII in 1937, the ware is found with his cypher and also that of George VI and Queen Elizabeth, substituted after Edward's abdication (Plate 70).
4725	*Coronation Ware* As for no. 4724, but with blue and white squares, the latter having central red dots. Tubed in blue (Plate 70).
4726	*Coronation Ware* As for no. 4724, but with purple squares and blue dots. Tubed in black.

No number *Coronation Ware* With the inscription HERE'S A HEALTH UNTO HIS MAJESTY 1937 tubed in blue, on a snow glaze ground. Possibly not commercially produced.

4794	Bands of stylised tulip and other flower-heads and lotus leaves tubed in blue and enamelled in pink, purple and blue. Finished in gold and bronze. Blue blown glaze. Introduced in 1936 (Plate 69).
4795	*Spanish Tree** Stylised tree tubed in brown with spiky leaves lustred and enamelled in orange and scarlet. Brown leaves and band at bottom of tree. Foot-line in scarlet and silver. Blown yellow glaze (Plate 66).
4825	*Spanish Tree** variation. As 4795 but green band and green leaves, shaded brown, at bottom of tree. Silver foot-line. Scarlet and silver lines at top.
4903	Variation of the *Stitch** and *Patch** patterns, the stitches tubed in black. Segmental circular central device, the left half enamelled in blue and the right in green, divided by a scarlet vertical stripe. Finished in primrose and green lustres (Plate 50).
4921	*Golden Leaves* Leaves and flowers in autumnal colours, with some leaves falling from their stems. Tubed in brown. Off-white ground. Also made with green leaves. Introduced in 1937 and one of Charlotte Rhead's most popular designs, it was produced in quantity. Revived after World War Two when it was known as *Falling Leaves*. This name also seems to have been used by some Richardson decorators in the 1930s (Plates 67 & 72).
4922	*Florian* Band of green pointed and lobed stylised leaf forms within an undulating ring of flower-heads with red rims and centres. Tubed in brown. Mottled green glaze (Plate 71). The design also appears with a snow glaze.
4923	Band of alternating interlocking silver and brown 'comma' shapes tubed in brown. Thin red and thick brown bands. Fawn glaze.
4924	*Carnation* Stylised carnation flowers tubed in blue with red and gold centres and light blue leaves. Snow glaze (Plate 73).
4925	*Arabian Scroll* Band of alternating green, scarlet and uncoloured scroll forms, tubed in black. Blue and orange bands and off-green glaze. Introduced in 1937 (Plate 74).
4926	*Arabian Scroll* As for no. 4925, but with alternating black and orange lustre, black and red lustre, or red and green lustre scrolls. Fawn glaze.
4953	*Foxglove* Foxglove plants tubed in blue, the flowers enamelled in pink, purple, blue, and green with green leaves and stems. Snow glaze. Undulating green border (Plate 76). This pattern, with no. 4954 (*Wisteria*), formed the centrepiece of the Richardson display at the British Industries Fair in February 1937 (Fig 40).
4954	*Wisteria* Stylised hanging wisteria flowers tubed in blue, and enamelled in pink, blue, orange and purple; brown stems; leaves in two shades of green. Snow glaze. Undulating green border (Plate 77). Queen Mary[23] bought a *Wisteria* pattern jug at the 1937 British Industries Fair, a development promptly advertised by the company at the event.
4957	*Arabian Scroll* As for no. 4925, but with alternating green and scarlet scrolls only. Tubed in brown.

4958	*Florian* As for no. 4922 but tubed in blue; flower centres enamelled in blue. Pink-purple lines between leaves. Finished in gold. Snow glaze.
4968	Interlocking bronze 'comma' shapes tubed in brown, the spaces between the shapes enamelled alternately in scarlet and black. Banded in brown with scarlet lines enclosing small tubed crosses. Mottled fawn glaze.
5049	*Florian* As for no. 4922 but tubed in brown with blue flower centres and green lustre leaves. Off-green mottled glaze.
5332	Small spray of four oval fruits enamelled in scarlet and yellow with two green leaves. Tubed stitch edge. Old gold and green mottled glaze.
5391	*Persian Leaf* Band of blue and purple spiky leaves with trailing stems and small round fruits enamelled in pink and orange. Rustic trellis. Mottled grey glaze (Plate 75).
5393	*Tudor Rose* Variation of no. 4040 (*Persian Rose*). Snow glaze ground with black and white flowers, their centres decorated with gold and white chequer patterns (Plate 65).
5411	*Caliph* Stylised flower-heads enamelled in pink, blue, scarlet and orange with leaves in two shades of green. Grey mottled glaze (Plate 81).
5623	*Tarragona* As for no. 5391 (*Persian Leaf*), but leaves enamelled in orange and yellow within bronze lustred bands. Tube-lined in grey under an off-white mottled glaze. Also found with leaves enamelled in orange or yellow only. This pattern was revived in 1951.
5627	*Tarragona* (or *Persian Leaf*) variation. As for no. 5623, but with orange and yellow leaves within green bands (Plate 79).
5728	Painted design as for no. 3727, but with band of pink leaves on a gold stem with wide bands of pink separated by thin gold bands. Grey mottled glaze (Plate 62). Later variations were tubed (nos. 6568 and 6668).
5802	*Fruit Border* Band of lustred orange and yellow fruits on brown stems and green leaves within a zig-zag border of leaf forms interspersed with red dots. Finished in bronze. Tubed in grey. Fawn glaze (Plate 82).
5803	*Palermo* Stylised flower-heads enamelled in red and mauve between trailing stems bearing clusters of small brown leaves. A variation (same pattern number) has dark pink lustred flowers and pink and brown leaves (Plates 80, 109 & 110). Advertised extensively in 1939.
5982	Circular fruits lustred in orange and brown, outlined with black tubed dashes. The fruits may also be green and yellow. Sprays of brown ribbed leaves. Mottled brown glaze (Plate 84).
5983	*Ankara* Stylised exotic flowers tubed in primula black, some with spiky petals and leaves, lustred in primrose, orange, green, blue and bronze, brown stems. Off-white ground. The pattern also appears in other colour combinations. Reintroduced in the 1950s (Plate 78).
6016	*Trellis* Undulating rustic trellis design tubed in brown, the panels enclosing a variety of plant forms and leaf sprays enamelled in pink, yellow, green, emerald, blue and purple. Mottled brown ground. Banded and finished in green. Introduced in 1939 (Plates 87 & 95).
6017	*Trellis* As for no. 6016, but finished in yellow.
6189	*Mexican* Four-petalled flower-heads tubed in brown and enamelled in scarlet, orange, black, green, blue and purple. Blue tulip-heads and stylised leaf forms (Plate 87). This pattern was revived after World War Two.
6198	*Basket* Chequer pattern basket containing three stylised flower-heads enamelled in scarlet, orange and blue. Basket and leaves lustred in black, brown and bronze. Tubed in brown. Mottled brown glaze. In production in 1940.
6353	Clusters of apples, some lustred in orange, primrose and green on lustred brown leafy branches within an undulating border. Tubed in brown. Mottled off-white glaze. This pattern also appears with the apples lustred in orange and primrose only. Perhaps also produced in the 1950s.

In addition to those patterns mentioned above, a few of Charlotte Rhead's other patterns were probably also produced after the end of World War Two. These include nos. 6568 and 6668 which are tubed versions of no. 3727. Some other designs may be based on patterns made by Charlotte Rhead before she left Richardson's, perhaps with different colour arrangements.

6564	Elongated stylised flower-heads, each with five pink lobed petals and dark pink centres, between uncoloured leaves on Y-shaped stems. Mottled grey glaze (Plate 85).
6568	As no. 3727, but with uncoloured leaves tubed in brown. White matt glaze (Plate 62).
6572	Stylised flowers tubed in brown on a yellow ground.
6668	As no. 3727, but with pink leaves tubed in brown and outlined in gold. Mottled cream glaze.
6778	Dull red and pink flower-heads on stems with pink and grey leaves within bands of dull red lotus leaves. Finished in gold. Grey or cream ground. A post-war version of no. 5983 (Plate 88).
6882	Dull red and pink open flower-heads and dull green leaves, finished in gold.

Other late tubed patterns, among them nos. 6569, 6572, 6828 (*Scroll Leaf*), 6884 (*Pink Oyster*) (Plate 89), 6904, 6917 (*Danube Spray*), 6927 (*Tulip Spray*) and 7377 (*Leaf and Trellis*) (Plates 84 & 108) do not appear to owe anything to Charlotte Rhead. A waterlily design (pattern number not known) is also the work of a post-war designer.

Backstamps
A.G.Richardson & Co. (Crown Ducal)

Backstamp 1 – Mark used from c1932 to c1938. Occasionally the word 'Ware' appears immediately under 'Crown Ducal' (c1932).

Backstamps 2 and 3 – Marks used from c1933 to c1938.

Backstamp 4 – Mark used from c1934 until c1961

CROWN DUCAL
MADE IN
ENGLAND

Backstamps 5 and 6 – Introduced c1936 and in use until c1961. A smaller version (right) sometimes appeared in colour.

Backstamp 7 – c1936 – c1942

As backstamp 7 but CROWN DUCAL omitted

CHAPTER SEVEN

H. J. Wood Ltd.

The firm of H. J. Wood Ltd. was established towards the end of the nineteenth century as an independent company by members of the Wood family. Although separate from the firm of Wood & Sons, the large and growing company run by Thomas Francis Wood and his son, Harry, H. J. Wood Ltd. had close ties with it, often using Wood's blanks for its productions. The firm was also based in Burslem at the Alexandra Pottery, close to the Wood & Sons Trent and New Wharf Potteries. This fraternal relationship continued until the late 1930s when the company ran into serious financial difficulties. From these it was extricated by Harry Wood who had succeeded his father as Chairman and Managing Director of Wood & Sons; though the company retained its name, it lost its independence and became just another part of the Wood empire.

This was the state of affairs when Charlotte Rhead left Richardson's, probably sometime towards the end of 1941. Harry Wood still controlled Wood & Sons and, although he was reaching his seventieth birthday, he continued to keep a tight grip on the affairs of the company which he had joined in 1889. He had always held the Rhead family in high regard and appreciated the vital part Frederick had played as art director from 1912 to 1929 in advancing the firm's reputation and successes. When Frederick left to join Cauldon Potteries, Harry Wood maintained a more than friendly interest in his welfare and during his final illness he came to see him each week, bringing fruit and flowers and putting his car and driver at his disposal so that he could get a change of air. So when Charlotte found herself out of a job, it was Harry Wood who came to her rescue by offering her work and accommodation at the H. J. Wood Alexandra Pottery. As was the case at Richardson's, her exact job at the Alexandra Pottery was not clear. The Wood's art director, Eddie Sambrook, had by then joined the armed forces and, in his absence Charlotte may have temporarily assumed his rôle – as the press and Dollie were to claim after her death.[1] But in the emergency conditions that prevailed at the time, production was very restricted. At first she may have been working on tableware alone, as the company records for July 1941 suggest, when she is known to have acid etched some designs. Soon no doubt she also started work on a new range of tube-lined wares for H. J. Wood, in anticipation of the time when production could be resumed.

There was doubtless an element of compassion in Harry Wood's decision to reemploy Charlotte, as the war imposed all sorts of restrictions on the manufacture of tube-lined wares. But Harry was a shrewd businessman and must have seen that there was likely to be a profit in his action, too. Besides he clearly enjoyed Charlotte's company. She evidently had a calming effect on him, and he would often come to her office for a chat, particularly when irritated by some mishap.

Production developed very slowly, and in 1943 one of the tube-liners who had worked for Charlotte at Richardson's turned down an offer of a job at H. J. Wood, doubting whether there was worthwhile employment there. Nevertheless, within a short time Charlotte seems to have produced some fifty patterns. The number of different designs was in fact much smaller, as many were simply colour variations and, of the original designs that were different, comparatively few ever went into general production. Most of those that did, some fifteen in all, were very successful and it was not until about 1960, some thirteen years after Charlotte's death, that production finally came to an end.

In the previous chapter it was observed that by 1938 Charlotte seemed to be running out of steam, and that her patterns were tending to become repetitive. Not that they were bad – she was far too good a designer for that, but somehow the inventive spark was lacking. So it is not surprising to find that many of her new patterns for H. J. Wood were reworkings of designs she had used in the 1930s, predominating motifs featuring flowers and fruit. She continued to favour 'broken' glazes too, especially the Greystone and Brownstone with their attractive mottled grey and brown effects. She also went on making extensive use of lustres, and patterns such as T.L.5 and T.L.76 (Plates 92 & 93) were remarkably successful. These lustres were thinly applied and they provided cheap but showy decorations. When at last they became available in Britain, they must have come as a welcome relief to the public, who had been restricted to undecorated 'utility' wares for so long.

Among the tableware exhibited by Wood's at the Britain Can Make It Exhibition in 1946 (rather unfairly

Fig 42 Advertisement for the 'Woodland' pattern (T.L. 82), March 1949.

Fig 43 The H. J. Wood tube-liners at work, Christmas 1947. Rose Platt is in the right hand corner. The large vase in the foreground, pattern T.L. 1, was, like the rest of the production at the time, made for export.

dubbed by the popular press the Britain Can't Have It Exhibition) was a design by Charlotte named *Woodland* (Fig 42). She added a stylised thin white tubed leaf decoration to the standard green *Beryl* body which Wood's had introduced just before the war. At first there were problems as the green body tended to stain the tubing, but these were eventually overcome, and the *Woodland* range turned out to be very popular. It was made in several colour combinations and was produced for some years.

During and immediately after the War, production of Charlotte's tube-lined wares was mainly aimed at the export markets (Fig 43). The largest of these were the United States and what were termed at the time the British Dominions, particularly Canada, Australia and New Zealand. Patterns which are seldom or never seen in Britain still turn up in the United States so the range, overall, must have been greater than would be expected from research in the United Kingdom. It would seem then that when the unrestricted sale of tube-lined wares was at last allowed in the home market, a conscious decision was taken to concentrate on a limited number of patterns. This decision may have been forced on Wood's by circumstances not of its making. By 1947 Charlotte herself had understood that her designs, with their 1930s motifs and decorations, were beginning to look old-fashioned. So she and Eddie Sambrook, who had returned to his post of art director after demobilisation, decided to try a new approach. Experimental pieces were developed in a manner reminiscent of the rich underglaze decorations of the 1920s, though it was now illegal to use the lead glazes which had been available at that time. But before these experiments could be concluded, Charlotte's cancer reappeared. This time there was to be no recovery and on 6th November 1947, she died at her home in Watlands Avenue, Wolstanton. As the new ware had not been developed sufficiently to allow for commercial production, the project was abandoned. A lamp base in this experimental ware is illustrated in Fig 44. Had Charlotte lived, the new line would surely have been a great success. Without Charlotte, however, Wood's had to make do largely with her established designs, though Eddie Sambrook and others did add a few new ones to the series, often in her style. In the circumstances the company must have felt it prudent to limit the size of the range, a decision which proved surprisingly successful.

During the last few months of her life Charlotte did much of her work at

Fig 44 H. J. Wood Ltd., experimental lamp base. In 1947 Charlotte Rhead and the art director, Eddie Sambrook, began working on a new range of designs. After she died in November that year, the project was abandoned.

home. She also had a visit from her sister Katherine, Sister St. Pierre. Now that the war was over, she was allowed by her religious order to come to England every year. Katherine was alarmed to see how ill her sister looked and sought out her doctor. He told her the true state of things and added that Charlotte had not looked after herself properly since her first attack of cancer. But if Charlotte neglected herself, she did not neglect her staff and one of her last acts was to negotiate a wage increase for the tube-liners, insisting, as always, that they should get the top decorators' rates. She is warmly remembered for that and for many other similar actions.

Dollie, now retired, inherited the house in Watlands Avenue and lived there until her own death in 1981. Production of Charlotte's designs for H. J. Wood continued until about 1960 and visitors to Dollie recall her outspoken criticism of the practice of attaching Charlotte's name to all the company's tube-lined productions, irrespective of who had designed them. Her annoyance outweighed her pleasure that her sister's last designs had turned out to be so popular and that her name had become a well-known hallmark for a whole range of wares. Charlotte herself, with her long experience of working for commercial potteries, would surely have approved.

Notes for collectors
Charlotte's designs for H. J. Wood were marketed under the old Bursley Ware label. The Crown Pottery, where Bursley Ware was originally produced, was taken over by Susie Cooper in the early 1930s, but Harry Wood had retained the Bursley company name. It seemed entirely appropriate that this should now be used for Charlotte's productions, and a new printed backstamp was devised which read: *Bursley Ware Charlotte Rhead England*. This backstamp was eventually applied to all Wood's tube-line productions, some of which were not Charlotte's designs, a fact which, as has already been noted, caused much irritatation to Dollie Rhead. Another backstamp, WOOD'S ARABESQUE *by Charlotte Rhead*, was also used, though less frequently. The significance of this second mark is not clear and pieces decorated with the same design can be found with either backstamp. Moreover Charlotte had given the name *Arabesque* to one specific pattern, number T.L.4.

In addition to the backstamp, which usually appears on all but the smallest items (these are just marked 'Made in England'), pieces may carry tube-liners' and decorators' marks and a pattern number. Some objects, too, have a shape number, the figures usually being impressed or embossed on the bases. The patterns are numbered in sequence, preceded by the letters T.L. and starting at 1. About 120 numbers were set aside for these tube-lined patterns, although some do not appear to have been used and of those that were, not all were Charlotte's work. The pattern book was discarded when the tube-lined range was discontinued, but fortunately parts of it, including some of Charlotte's own illustrations and notes, were preserved. The list of patterns that follows has been compiled from observation, from the surviving pages of the pattern book, from a catalogue issued in about 1954 (Plate 90) and from discussions with people who worked for Wood's at the time – in particular Eddie Sambrook, the art director. Gaps in the sequence of T.L. numbers suggest that those designs, if they were ever realised, were not commercially produced.

Charlotte's designs were applied to a great range of shapes and objects: plaques, flower jugs, wall pockets, lamp bases, bowls, trays, ashtrays, trinket sets and vases, many of them quite small.

H. J. Wood Ltd. Decorators
Tube-liners and their marks
A   Shirley Arkenstall ?
E
F
I   May Powell
.I.   Jessie Hazelhurst
J
M
O   Mrs Walker
R   Rose Platt
S   Clara Stevenson ?
X   Emmie Morris

H. J. Wood Ltd. Patterns

No information is available about several of the H. J. Wood (T.L.) pattern numbers. Presumably they were either not used or were allocated to patterns that were not commercially produced. They have been omitted from the following list. A catalogue issued in about 1954 illustrated several of these designs, presumably the more popular items in the T.L. range (Plate 90).

Pattern Number

T.L.1   Zigzag bands of thin spiky leaves overlaying a wider lobed zigzag band, lustred in shades of orange, green and brown. Mottled brown glaze. A reworking, with minor changes, of Richardson pattern no. 2682 (Plate 49).

T.L.2   Sprays of three green leaves between sprays of three heart-shaped yellow and orange leaves. Mottled white glaze (Plate 91). Illustrated in Wood's catalogue c1954.

T.L.3   *Trellis* A rustic trellis design with stylised open flower-heads, lustred in yellow and orange with green chequered centres, on leafy stems. Mottled brown glaze. Illustrated in a Wood's catalogue of c1954. The pattern is also known with pink and mauve lustred flower-heads and pink lustred leaves (Plates 95 & 96).

T.L.4   *Arabesque* Hydrangea flowers in blue, red and mauve with brown leaves, some falling from their stems (Plate 92). Illustrated in Wood's catalogue c1954. The design incorporates elements from two Richardson patterns, no. 3797 *Hydrangea*, and no. 4921 *Golden Leaves*.

T.L.5   Orange and yellow lustred fruits, perhaps peaches or pomegranates, on fruiting boughs with stylised blue and pink flower-heads and small circular seeds (Plate 92). Illustrated in a Wood's catalogue of c1954. Incorporates motifs from several Richardson patterns including no. 3321, *Granada*.

T.L.8   Gold polka dots on an ivory ground. Also made in other colours. Illustrated in the Wood's catalogue of c1954 on a lamp base with a pink ground.

T.L.10   Stylised design of exotic fruit and flowers enamelled in violet and blue; mottled grey glaze. Perhaps not commercially produced.

T.L.12   Bands of scrolling foliage, tubed in solid blue, alternating with solid blue heart-shaped and circular devices with chequered centres. This design appears to have been applied mainly to lamp bases (Plate 91).

T.L.14   Multi-coloured plant design with tulips and stylised flower-heads, sometimes between bands of blue and mauve ribbons. Cream ground (Plates 93, 111 & 112). Illustrated in Wood's catalogue c1954.

T.L.18   Stylised fish with leaf-shaped fins and tail on a chequered body, tubed in black and enamelled pale green. This pattern, and its variations (T.L.19 and 20) were probably not commercially produced.

T.L.19   Similar to T.L.18 but enamelled flesh pink.

T.L.20   Similar to T.L.18 but enamelled emerald green.

T.L.27   Yellow and green chrysanthemum flowers tubed in black. Jade green ground.

T.L.28   Similar to T.L.27 but with pink ground. Illustrated in Wood's catalogue c1954 on a lamp base.

T.L.29   Similar to T.L.27 but with pink flowers and green ground.

T.L.30   Similar to T.L.27 but with heliotrope flowers and marigold ground.

T.L.31   Rustic panels enclosing stylised star shapes surrounded by circular fruits on a pink or buff mottled ground alternating with spirals on a mottled white ground. Enamelled in grey and pink or orange and yellow (Plate 100).

T.L.32   As for T.L.31, but enamelled in light green and grey.

T.L.33   As for T.L.31, but enamelled in mid-green and grey.

T.L.37   *Daisy.* Open daisy flowers tubed in brown and enamelled in various colours (Plates 91 & 113). This pattern is known in several colour combinations.

T.L.38   Similar to T.L.5, but enamelled in brighter colours with leaves in two shades of green. Illustrated in Wood's catalogue c1954.

T.L.39   Overlapping semi-circles enclosing stylised fruiting stems or stylised fruit clusters. Cream ground. The same pattern number was later used for a tube-lined stylised multi-coloured leaf design with stylised blue flower-heads. The latter was not designed by Charlotte Rhead and was presumably introduced after her death (Plate 118)

T.L.40   Stylised carnations flowers and leaves tubed in solid dark blue with details picked out in gold. Mottled grey glaze (Plates 92 & 116). Also known tubed in light blue or black. Illustrated in Wood's catalogue c1954.

T.L.40C As for T.L.40 but with carmine red carnations and leaves. Gold finish (Plate 120).

T.L.41   Stylised poppy seed-heads with chequered centres in red and black. Spiky blue leaves.

T.L.42   Apples, pears and grapes on leafy stems enamelled underglaze.

T.L.43   Wind-tossed peony flowers and leaves outlined in blue against a background of circular fruits in blue or purple. Mottled grey glaze (Plate 104). Illustrated in Wood's catalogue c1954.

T.L.51   Stylised flower and leaf design enamelled in several colours. Mottled green ground.

T.L.53   Groups of comma shaped forms tubed in brown, some lustred pink on a pink ground. This design appears to have been applied mainly to lamp-bases.

T.L.60   Band of painted black spirals between smaller bands of black S-shapes. Dark brown ground. Possibly made for export only.

T.L.61   Similar to T.L.60 but with light brown ground.

T.L.63   Similar to T.L.60 but with green ground.

T.L.65 Blue dragon amid cloud scrolls and other Chinese forms; sometimes finished in gold. This design can be compared with the popular Richardson pattern *Manchu* (no. 4511) which was produced in green (Plate 68).

T.L.68 Variation of T.L.43.

T.L.69 Dragon similar to T.L.65 with brown sgraffito border designed by Eddie Sambrook.

T.L.71 Similar to T.L.60, but with printed design.

T.L.72 Similar to T.L.61, but with printed design

T.L.74 Similar to T.L.63, but with printed design.

T.L.75 Design of grapes, pomegranates and flowers.

T.L.76 Wind-tossed tulips enamelled and lustred in pink and violet with spiky and lobed green leaves and stylised prunus blossom between bands decorated with geometric devices. Mottled grey glaze (Plate 93). Illustrated in Wood's catalogue c1954.

T.L.82 *Woodland*. Running band of narrow stylised leaves, punctuated by dots and tubed in white on a green *Beryl* body (Fig. 42). The pattern was shown by Wood's at the 1946 Britain Can Make It exhibition. Also tubed in feather blue (T.L.82B), matt blue (T.L.83), green (T.L.82G), and pink (T.L.84). In another variation the tubing was covered with best liquid gold, but this was probably only used on lamp bases.

T.L.85 As for T.L.65, but dragon tubed in white. Crimson glaze. Sometimes finished with gold bands.

Other T.L. patterns were mainly the work of the art director, Eddie Sambrook or, in a few instances, junior designers. However some of Charlotte Rhead's designs were produced in different colours, perhaps after her death. They include the following:

T.L.97 Similar to T.L.2, but with leaves in lighter green. Mottled grey glaze.

T.L.99 Similar to T.L.40, but tubed in black or grey. White matt glaze. No gold embellishment.

T.L.99G As for T.L.99, but finished in liquid gold.

T.L.100 Similar to T.L.40, but with only the outline tubed in black. Enamelled in black with white matt glaze. No gold embellishment.

T.L.100A As for T.L.100, but finished in liquid gold.

T.L.101 As for T.L.8, but with red polka dot decoration.

T.L.114 As for T.L.1, but with brighter colours and high gloss glaze.

Backstamps H. J. Wood Ltd

Backstamp 1 – normal mark – c1943-c1960

Backstamp 2 – Arabesque – c1943–c1960

Backstamp 3 – mark used for small items c1943–c1960.

CHAPTER EIGHT

Price Guide and Auction Trends

Prices of ceramics designed by Charlotte Rhead have remained remarkably stable over the past ten years and her work is still cheap when compared with that of Clarice Cliff and Susie Cooper. This is surprising as the designs themselves often show a degree of sophistication lacking in those of other designers, while tube-lining, Charlotte's speciality, is a relatively difficult technique and a more expensive one than ordinary painting. Perhaps because of the comparatively low prices which her designs command, there are at present no specialist auctions of her work, though pieces can often be found in general sales, especially those relating to the inter-war years. It can be expected that prices will show some increase in the future. Prices of Frederick Rhead's designs for Wood's have also remained on the low side, though these too may rise.

Wood and Sons and Bursley Ltd. productions are relatively uncommon. They can be striking and colourful, no doubt partly due to the lead glazes which were still permitted at the time. For this reason these 1920s productions tend to fetch higher prices that the popular Crown Ducal wares of the 1930s or those of H. J. Wood Ltd. after World War Two.

In general the price reflects the condition of any particular piece. Lustres, in particular, were subject to wear, as are some onglaze enamel colours. A restoration, too, however skilfully carried out, will also materially effect the price.

Tiles

Tiles tubed by Charlotte Rhead appear on the market only rarely and in consequence command relatively high prices. A framed standard sized tile of around 17cm. square can be expected to cost between £600 -£900/$1170-$1755, depending on the design. Smaller tiles, 16x8 cm., may fetch between £300-£500/$585-$975.

Wood & Sons

Printed Patterns for Ornamental Wares

Simple designs on vases, flower tubes and bowls, blue or black print
e.g. *Brocade, Caliph, Oriental Birds, Chung, Kang Hi, Formosa*   £40-£100/$80-$195

Coloured designs on vases, bowls, and jardinières
e.g. *Arras, Sheraton, Chung, Kang Hi* and *Korea*   £60-£250/$115-$490
Plaques e.g. *Mikado, Shan Tung*   £300-£500/$585-$975

Pâte-sur-Pâte

Flower tubes, vases and bowls, depending on size   £300-£700/$585-$1365

Tube-lined wares designed by Frederick Rhead

Elers and *Trellis*
Small pieces including. boxes, items from trinket sets,
bottles, candlesticks   £100-£200/$195-$390
Vases, jardinières, ginger jars, complete trinket sets.   £250-£500/$490-$975
Toilet sets.   £300-£600/$585-$1170

Tube-lined wares designed by Charlotte Rhead

Plaques, seated Japanese female figures.   £1000+/$1950
Vases, flower tubes.   £200-£400/$390-$780
Bursley Ware (Rhodian, Seed Poppy)
Vases, bottles, according to size   £200-£700/$390-$1365

Bursley Ltd.

Printed Patterns
Round and octagonal vases and bowls, bottles,
ash trays, biscuit barrels, according to size.   £50-£400/$100-$780

Numbered Patterns
Tube-lined wares
All Bursley Ltd. tube-lined wares are relatively uncommon. The patterns most frequently found are the Wood's Bursley Ware *Seed Poppy*, which reappears as Bursley Ltd. pattern no. 28, pattern 324 and *Pomona* (pattern 456). The rarity of a particular design, however, has not so far materially affected its price.

Toilet sets, if more or less complete	£400-£600/$780-$1170
Ash trays, jugs, chamber pots and other items from toilet or trinket sets, tea and coffee sets, candlesticks, according to size	£80-£450/$155-$880
Vases, bowls, bottles according to size	£200-£600/$390-$1170
Plaques	£300-£700/$585-$1365

Printed Wares

Plates, cups and saucers and ashtrays	£30-£60/$60-$115
Jugs, tea and coffee pots and sets, vases, bowls, candlesticks, according to size	£50-£300/$100-$585
Plaques	£200-£400/$390-$780

Cosy Pots

Tubed pots (*Trellis*, *Seed Poppy*, pattern 726), complete with lids	£60-£250/$115-$490
Without lids	£40-£200/$80-$390
Plain and printed pots	£25-£100/$50-$195

Ellgreave Pottery

Lottie Rhead Ware, tableware, cups, saucers and jugs	£20-£50/$40-$100
Ellgreave printed floral designs, vases and bowls	£40-£70/$80-$135

Burgess & Leigh

Surprisingly, Charlotte Rhead's designs for Burgess & Leigh are relatively uncommon, though her output for the firm must have been substantial. As with her Wood's and Bursley Ltd. productions, the rarity of some patterns is not at present reflected in their prices. Exceptionally, a few elaborate plaques which were probably tubed by Charlotte herself, can be expected to fetch prices in the region of £1000/$1950 or more. These include patterns 4011, 4012 , 4013 and 4111. An example of the latter, decorated with a richly dressed young woman holding a bunch of grapes in front of a parrot, has sold for £2700/$5265, the highest price recorded so far for a design by Charlotte Rhead.

As prices for the remainder of the Burgess & Leigh range are in general modest, no distinction is made in the list that follows as between the relatively common and the rarer designs.

Vases

Small	£75-£200/$145-$390
Medium	£150-£300/$295-$585
Large	£250-£600/$490-$1170

Bowls

Small	£50-£150/$100-$295
Medium, some with embossed leaves	£200-£400/$390-$780

Fruit Sets
Serving bowl and 6 small bowls £200-£400/$390-$780
Single small bowl £40-£80/$80-$155

Sandwich Sets
Dishes of various shapes: fan, square, long (*Richmond shape*),
round or crescent with four or six plates £200-£400/$390-$780
Single dishes £50-£120/$100-$235
Single plates £25-£80/$50-$155

Plaques
Plaques in addition to those listed above according to size £200-£700/$390-$1365
and pattern.

Tableware
Burgess & Leigh tableware designed by Charlotte Rhead with tube-lined or printed decoration is uncommon although many different items were manufactured and in a range of sizes. Prices therefore are likely to be volatile depending on the size and utility of the piece.
Tea and coffee pots and associated wares,
particularly in sets, command higher prices £20-£500/$39-$975

Children's Ware
Usually found with printed designs but similar tubed designs are also reported
to be known. £30-£100/$60-$195

A.G.Richardson (Crown Ducal)

As with Wood's and Burgess & Leigh productions, the rarity of a particular Crown Ducal design does materially increase its value. The commonest patterns, the simple *Stitch* and *Patch* and their variations, which were decorated by the junior paintresses and apprentices and are unmarked with a Rhead facsimile signature, are the cheapest of the Richardson wares. These simple decorations were used for a great variety of objects including vases, jugs, flower jugs, plates and plaques.
Examples are common. £40-£120/$80-$235

Vases and Flower Jugs (other than *Stitch* and *Patch*)
Plain
Small £60-£150/$115-$295
Medium £100-£250/$195-$490
Large £200-£400/$390-$780
Wall pockets and vases £50-£250/$100-$490

Complex Vases with handles
Small £80-£180/$155-$350
Medium £120-£280/$235-$545
Large £220-£600/$430-$1170

Bowls
Small £50-£150/$100-$295
Medium £80-£200/$155-$390
Large £100-£250/$195-$490

Plaques

Small (10", 12")	£125-£250/$245-$490
Medium (14", 16")	£200-£400/$390-$780
Large (18")	£300-£600/$585-$1170

Plaques can also be found with unusual designs and no pattern numbers. These were probably samples that may not have been commercially produced. Such pieces can command higher prices.

Tea and Coffee Wares

Teapots and Coffee pots	£60-£200/$115-$390
Coffee cans and saucers, sets of six	£100-£200/$195-$390
Coffee cans, single	£20-£40/$39-$80

Children's Ware

Plates, saucers, cups and mugs	£25-£100/$50-$195

Table Lamps

Without shades	£125-£250/$245-$490
With matching shades, depending on condition	£150-£300/$295-$585

H. J. Wood Ltd.

Vases and Flower Jugs

Small	£40-£80/$80-$155
Medium	£75-£150/$145-$295
Large	£100-£250/$195-$490
Wall pockets and vases	£40-£120/$80-$235

Bowls

Small	£40-£80/$80-$155
Medium	£60-£120/$115-$235
Large	£80-£150/$155-$295

Plaques

10", 12"	£100-£175/$195-$340
14", 16"	£150-£250/$295-$490
18", 20"	£200-£300/$390-$585

Miscellaneous

Ginger Jars	£50-£200/$100-$390
Ash trays	£15-£50/$29-$100
Sweet dishes	£15-£50/$29-$100
Cigarette boxes	£50-£100/$100-$195
Trinket Sets (often incomplete)	£50-£200/$100-$390
Baskets, small	£30-£50/$60-$100
Baskets, large	£40-£60/$80-$120

Tea Wares

Teapots	£40-£80/$80-$155
Milk jugs and sugar bowls	£20-£40/$39-$80
Cake plates and stands	£50-£100/$100-$195

Table Lamps

Large	£60-£150/$115-$295
Medium	£40-£130/$80-$255

With matching shades, prices increase according to condition

Woodland (Pattern T.L.82 and variations)

Woodland was primarily a tableware range. It was also used to decorate a variety of associated items, including rose and posy bowls, trays, ash trays, sweet dishes, comports and cheese dishes.

The price reflect the size and utility of the object offered £20-£200/$39-$390

Notes

Chapter One: The Rhead Family
1. G. W. and F. A. Rhead, *Staffordshire Pots and Potters*, London, 1906, p. 348.
2. *Pottery and Glass Trades Review* V.1, 1877-78, p. 223.
3. Wedgwood letter book; archive 2698-4.
4. *Pâte-sur-pâte* was a decorative technique applied to a porcelain body. A cameo-like effect was built up by the application of many very thin layers of porcellaneous slip. Each layer had to be completely dry and finished with a carving tool before the next could be applied. When the piece was fired, the decoration became translucent.
5. This must be the bottle seen by George Bedford of the Watcombe Terra-Cotta Co. at the Exhibition about which he wrote: 'A very rich effect was produced by a head in profile in buff clay on a red ground, the elaborate Egyptian head-dress being executed in the same colours . . .' *The Society of Arts Artisan Reports on the Paris Universal Exhibition 1878*, (London, Sampson Low, 1879) p.90.
6. The vase, on loan from Sir William Gladstone, is normally on display in the Gladstone Pottery Museum, Longton, Stoke-on-Trent.
7. The pattern books are now in the Royal Doulton archives, Burslem.

Chapter Two: Charlotte Rhead and her Brothers and Sisters
1. Letter from F. A. Rhead to William Moorcroft, 10 December 1906. I am grateful to Beatrice Moorcroft for bringing this letter to my attention.
2. Information from Mrs. Platt who worked as a tube-liner at Burgess & Leigh and H. J. Wood.
3. Undated typescript, Museum of Ceramics, East Liverpool, Ohio.
4. Information from the late Mary Harper who worked at Bootes with Charlotte Rhead. She thought Charlotte only stayed for about two months and that she also worked for Marsden's, another tile manufacturer.
5. Information from the late Ernest Bailey, a former modeller at Burgess & Leigh.
6. *PGR* August 1937, p.220.
7. G. Woolliscroft Rhead, *Modern Practical Design*, (London, Batsford, 1912), p. 2.
8. Lecture on 'Decoration as applied to clay ware', 21 September 1921, reported in *PG* November 1921,
9. Lecture on 'A pottery designer's views on art', 3 December 1921, reported in *PG* January 1922, p.83.
10. *PG* December 1947, p.1012.

Chapter Three: The Rheads as Tile Designers and Decorators
1. *PGR* June 1923, p.477.
2. The articles, published in *PGR*, ran from July 1922 until February 1924.
3. Ibid. p. 479.
4. Cox's Potteries Annual and Year Book, 1924, p.83.
5. '... both Dolly and Lottie were doing tube lining on tiles. Some of the tiles were decorated and painted by father and then tube-lined by Lottie or Dolly and framed they made beautiful pictures to hang on the walls.' Katherine Rhead (Sister St.Pierre), undated and unpaginated manuscript, The family of Frederick Alfred Rhead, (Sampans?, [Jura, France] , c1980s), private collection. At this point in the manuscript Katherine Rhead was referring to the period around 1901/1902.
6. Idem.
7. Ibid. 'Father painted a lovely picture of Tax...'. This painting was no doubt copied by Lottie or Dollie.
8. In another undated manuscript (private collection), pp.11-12, Katherine Rhead claimed: 'He [the German, Theimeicke] persuaded father to have a factory of his own and he would be a partner. It was a complete failure. The German went back to Germany and left father with a tremendous debt to pay. Father was entirely ruined...'
9. Ibid. p. 12. According to Katherine Rhead her elder sister Marie decided to get married in 1911 while her father was in America. She observed: 'Marie took possession of... the tube-line tiles to decorate her new house'.

Chapter Four: Wood & Sons Bursley Ltd., The Ellgreave Pottery Co.
1. *PG* March 1912, p.273.
2. Information from the late Mary Harper, a former decorator at Bootes and Burgess & Leigh.
3. *PG* July 1911 p.781.
4. 'Pounce' is explained in the Appendix.
5. *PGR* March 1919, p.176.
6. *PG* April 1919, p.360.
7. The registration of Bursley Ltd. was reported in *PG* December 1920, p.1665. The directors of the company included F. A. Rhead.
8. The registration of Ellgreave Ltd. was reported in *PG* August 1921, p.1231.
9. Department of Overseas Trade, *International Exhibition of Modern and Industrial Arts, Paris British Section April – October MCMXXV*, p.93. On page 103 of this catalogue, the Wood exhibit, which was displayed alongside that of Bursley Ltd, was described as consisting of 'Specialities in Dinner Ware, Hotel Ware and General Domestic Pottery for all markets'.
10. Gordon M. Forsyth was Director of Instruction at the Potteries' Art Schools.
11. *Report on the Present Position and Tendency of the Industrial Arts as indicated at the International Exhibition of Modern and Industrial Arts, Paris, 1925*, London, 1927, p.133.
12. *The Staffordshire Sentinel*, 21 August 1926 and *PG* September 1926, p.1418.
13. On the other hand much of Charlotte's work for the Ellgreave Pottery was marked *Lottie Rhead Ware*.
14. The tube-liner Katie Wall in conversation with the author.
15. *PGR* January 1929, p.19.
16. See also Bernard Bumpus, "The Perfect thing for Tea", *Collector's World*, April/May 1988, pp 34-35.
17. According to *PG* 1 December 1913, p. 1381: 'The "Orion" ware is carried out in a range of coloured dips, with the pattern printed and enamelled in suitable colours.'
18. *P. G.* March, 1926, p.573. The design was described as 'exclusive'.
19. *P. G.* Jan. 1927, p.75. The report went on: 'this seems to offer every prospect of being a particularly good seller'.
20. *P. G.* March, 1927, p.88.

Chapter Five: Burgess & Leigh

1 *P.G* March 1927, p.375.
2 *PG* September 1928, p.1417.
3 See Maureen Batkin, *Gifts for Good Children* Part II, p.51. Batkin refers to the wares as 'tube-lined' and also illustrates patterns nos.4419, 4420 and 4421 and *Quack Quack*, pattern no. 4766. The illustration also included designs featuring two other animals, lambs (*Baa-Baa*) and brown rabbits (*Bunny and Bed-Time*). The pattern numbers are not known. In addition she mentions, but does not illustrate, *Gee Gee*, described as a wooden horse on wheels.

Chapter Six: A. G. Richardson (Crown Ducal)

1 *PG* . November 1 1932, p.1390. I am grateful to Gerrard Shaw for drawing my attention to this report and its implications.
2 At the time, Forsyth was Director of Art Instruction at the Potteries' Art Schools.
3 Ibid. p. 1390.
4 Ibid. p. 1391
5 *PG* . March, 1927, p.375.
6 I am grateful to Eddie Sambrook for this interesting point.
7 George Woolliscroft Rhead, Studies in Plant Form London, Batsford, 1903.
8 *PG* Directory and Diary 1935, p.10. The pottery was also mentioned in an advertisement in P. G. Sept. 1934 (p.1041). I am grateful to Gerrard Shaw for pointing out that it took the company some time to effect the conversion.
9 Manuscript notes by Charlotte Rhead on patterns now in the Homer Laughlin China Company, Newell, West Virginia. Undated.
10 *PGR* August 1937, p.220.
11 Idem.
12 F. H. Rhead day-book, December 18th, 1936 "Went to Pittsburgh to see stores. Saw Crown Ducal 'snow' glaze." Homer Laughlin China Company, Newell, West Virginia.
13 *PG* Directory and Diary 1936, p.37.
14 Letter, Mrs. Rhead to F. H. Rhead, 23 March 1937.
15 Idem.
16 *PG* August 1937, p.1059.
17 At the time Harry Rhead was a Director of the Standard Tile Company, Zanesville, Ohio.
18 Letter, Dollie Rhead to F. H. Rhead, 21 July 1937.
19 Entries for July 1942 in a Wood's Section Book includes several tableware designs by 'Miss Rhead'. Three of these are marked 'Miss Rhead acid' so Charlotte had evidently etched the copper plates before the designs were engraved. This suggests that she had already been working for Wood's for at least six months.
20 An advertisement in an unidentified American trade magazine (c1934) reads "Maddock & Miller, Inc., have just brought out a new extra large size salad bowl and matching tray, as illustrated". The accompanying photograph is of a bowl and tray in the *Blossom* design. The copy continued: 'These are shown in 12 different decorations all in underglaze enamels. They are stocked.' In addition to *Blossom* and its variations, the twelve decorations may have included patterns 3169, 3170, 3191, 3259 and 3260, all of which are rarely found in Britain. This suggests that these were indeed produced mainly for the American market, as the advertisement claims. In addition bowls and trays in the standard tableware patterns 3048, 3049, 3050 and 3051 may also have been made for this market. These 'extra large size salad bowls' were described as 'punch bowls' in the Richardson pattern books.
21 The quotation is taken from the first edition of Edward Fitzgerald's translation of The Rubáiyát of Omar Khayyám (quatrain XI).
22 'As for the ornamental wares, there was one treatment which was admired by practically every dealer who visited the [Richardson's] stand. This emulated to some extent a kind of patchwork effect . . .', *PG*, April 1935, p. 517.
23 *PG*, April 1937, p. 550. The Queen is reported to have remarked that 'the snow glaze was in very good style'.

Chapter Seven: H. J. Wood Ltd.

1 In two short obituary notices Charlotte was described as 'art director of Wood & Sons, Ltd., Burslem' (*Stoke-on-Trent City Times*, Nov. 14 1947, p.1 and *PG* Dec. 1947, p.1012). Dollie Rhead also described her sister as 'art director at Wood & Sons' in a letter, dated October 25 1968, to an American correspondent who had enquired about the family. This letter is in a private collection in the United States.

Tube-lining

Tube-lining is a method of pottery decoration which makes use of a technique similar to that of icing a cake. A bag containing liquid clay (slip) is squeezed through a narrow glass tube on to the article to be decorated. This graphic line is attractive in itself and it also prevents the colours and lustres used for the decoration from running into each other.

The pattern might be applied in various ways. The tube-liner could carry it out in freehand, following a model prepared by the designer; Frederick Rhead's *Elers* and *Trellis* patterns were executed in this way (Plates 7 and 9). Another method required the tube-liner to follow a pattern which had been marked out in pencil on the object to be decorated. Charlotte Rhead preferred her tube-liners to use a 'pounce'. She would first draw the pattern on a sheet of tracing paper. The paper would then be placed over a piece of flannel and a number of small holes punched along the lines to be tubed. The perforated paper formed the pounce which would then be put on the object to be decorated and rubbed over with a pad dipped in soot. The pounce was then removed, leaving a row of black dots which would act as guide for the tube-liner to follow. Some pieces, such as vases, needed to be pounced twice, back and front. The sooty black dots would burn away when the article was fired. The manufacturer supplied the rubber bags for the slip, but the tube-liners were expected to provide their own glass tubes and to draw them out to the required width over a Bunsen burner.

Tube-lining could be applied directly to the unfired clay, which had to be leather-hard, or to biscuit ware which had already been fired. When applied to the biscuit a flux had to be added to the slip. Many of the tube-liners preferred to work on clay and that was the method normally used at Richardson's in the 1930s.

The cake-icing simile for tube-lining is the time honoured one and was used by the Rheads themselves. It is also misleading in that tube-lining is a highly skilled technique, requiring considerable control and dexterity. In the United States the process is sometimes known as the 'squeeze-bag' technique.

Select Bibliography

Books

Austerwick, J and B, *The Decorated Tile* , London, Pitman House, 1980.

Barnard, Julian, *Victorian Ceramic Tiles*, London, Cassell, 1979.

Batkin, Maureen, *Gifts for Good Children* Part II , Shepton Beauchamp, Richard Dennis, n.d. [1995].

Buckley, Cheryl, *Potters and Paintresses*, London, Women's Press, 1990.

Bumpus, Bernard, *Pâte-sur-Pâte The Art of Ceramic Relief Decoration, 1849-1992*, London, Barrie and Jenkins, 1992.

Bunt, C. G. E., *British Potters and Pottery Today*, Leigh-on-Sea, F. Lewis, 1956.

Knight, Richard and Hill, Susan, *Wileman*, Stratford Upon Avon, Jazz Publications, 1995.

Rhead, G. W. and F. A., *Staffordshire Pots and Potters*, London, Hutchinson, 1906. Republished, Wakefield, E.P.Publishing, 1977.

Rhead, G. W., *British Pottery Marks*, London, Scott, Greenwood and Co., 1910.

Spours, Judy, *Art Deco Tableware*, London, Ward Lock, 1988.

Watkins, Chris, Harvey, William and Senft, Robert, *Shelley Potteries*, London, Barrie and Jenkins, 1980, reprinted, 1986.

Thesis

Shaw, Gerrard, *A History of A. G. Richardson's Crown Ducal tableware production 1920-1940 and an assessment of its place in the progressive approach to design witnessed in the Staffordshire pottery industry in the inter-war years*,
M.A. Dissertation, University of Central England, 1993.

Exhibition Catalogue

Bumpus, Bernard, *Rhead Artists and Potters 1870-1950*, Geffrye Museum, London, 1986.

Articles

Bumpus, Bernard, *Tube-line Variations*, The Antique Collector, December 1985, pp.59-61.

Bumpus, Bernard, *America's Greatest Potter?*, The Antique Collector, April 1986, pp.38-43.

Davis, Chester, *The AETCO Tiles of Walter Crane*, Spinning Wheel, June 1973, pp18-20.

Periodicals

The Pottery Gazette (later *The Pottery Gazette and Glass Trades Review*).

The Pottery and Glass Record (after 1945 *Pottery and Glass*).

The Staffordshire Sentinel (after 1929 *The Evening Sentinel*).

Francis Joseph
P U B L I C A T I O N S
'The Collectors' Choice'

Detailed price and information books on 20th century ceramics and glass with galleries of extensive colour photographs in each. All the collector needs for identifying the wide range of valuable ceramics and glass produced over the past 100 years.

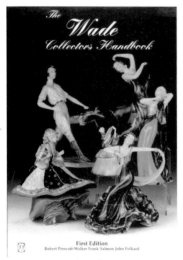

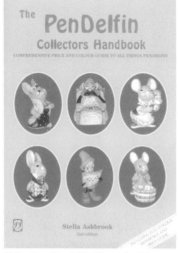

Wade Collectors Handbook

First edition on this much sought after pottery. Hugely popular, this book lists all the most collectable pieces. Everything from whimsies to figures. **£12.95**

Collecting Pendelfin Second edition

This second edition is bigger, brighter, better. Full of pictures and a mine of information on one of the UKs best known and best loved collectables. Full of new information and up to date prices. **£16.95**

Collecting Shelley Pottery

Comprehensive and wide-reading first edition on one of the UKs leading and most tasteful potteries. Hundreds of colour pictures plus prices. **£16.95**

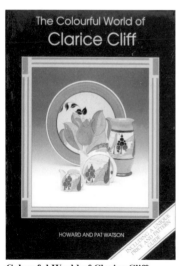

Colourful World of Clarice Cliff

Full colour book with up-to-date prices and hundreds of photographs. This book is ideal for all collectors and dealers alike. **£16.95**

Character Jug Collectors Handbook

Sixth Edition. Complete colour and price guide listing of all discontinued models. All Royal Doulton are listed along with other potteries. **£14.95**

The Bunnykins & Beatrix Potter Handbook

Price, picture and rarity guide of this now major collecting area. Royal Doulton, Beswick and Royal Albert all featured. Colour photographs throughout. **£14.95**

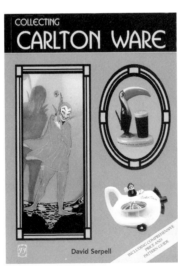
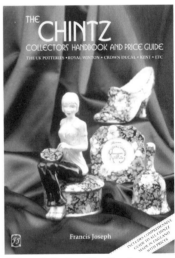

Notes

Notes

Notes

Notes

Notes